A MAN to MATCH the MOUNTAIN

A MAN to MATCH the MOUNTAIN

Overcoming The Obstacles of Life

David Roper

A Man to Match the Mountain
Copyright © 1996 David Roper

Discovery House Publishers is affiliated with RBC Ministries, Grand Rapids, Michigan 49512.

Discovery House books are distributed to the trade by Thomas Nelson Publishers, Nashville, Tennessee 37214.

Unless otherwise noted, all Scripture quotations are taken from the HOLY BIBLE: NEW INTERNATIONAL VERSION. Copyright © 1973, 1978, 1984 International Bible Society. Used by permission of Zondervan Publishing House.

Library of Congress Cataloging-in-Publication Data

Roper, David, 1933-
    A man to match the mountain : overcoming the obstacles of life / by David Roper.
        p.   cm.

    ISBN 1-57293-013-6

    1. Men—Religious life. 2. Bible. O.T.—Biography. I. Title.
BV4528.2.R66 1996
248.8'42—dc20   96-33524
                                                                        CIP

Printed in the United States of America

96 97 98 99 00 01 /CHG/ 10 9 8 7 6 5 4 3 2 1

CONTENTS

Great things are done when men and mountains meet;
This is not done by jostling in the street.

—William Blake

INTRODUCTION

God made him, and therefore let him pass for a man.

—William Shakespeare

I suppose by now everyone knows Robert Bly, the award-winning poet and guru of the current Men's Movement.

The source book of the movement, which Bly wrote, is called *Iron John,* the basis of which is a fairy tale by the same name inspired by Jacob and Wilhelm Grimm.

Iron John begins with strange happenings in a corner of the forest near a certain king's castle. Hunters go into the grove and never return. Others go after them and disappear. In time, people get the feeling there's something odd going on, and they don't venture into the woods anymore.

One day a visiting hunter shows up at the castle looking for something difficult and dangerous to do. The king says, "Well, there's this strange thing going on in our forest: people go in there and never come out."

"Fear is something I pay no attention to," the young man replies and, intrepid fellow that he is, hies himself into the woods with his dog.

Presently, the dog picks up the scent of game and goes in pursuit, arriving within a few minutes at the edge of a deep pool. A naked arm snakes out of the water, grabs the dog and pulls it down. The young man thinks, *This must be the place!*

He then goes back to the castle, rounds up a few other men and comes back to the pond to bucket out the water. It's hard work, but eventually they get to the bottom of things.

There on the floor of the pond they find a huge Wild Man, whose body is as brown as rusty iron, covered with hair from head to foot. The men capture him, tie him up, and lead him back to the castle where the king puts him in an iron cage and gives him the name, Iron John.

Bly finds an ancient truth in this tale: it speaks of a man looking down into the deep water of his soul and finding at the bottom a gruff, elemental Man. "What I am proposing," Bly once said, "is that every modern male has, lying at the bottom of his psyche, a large man covered with hair down to his feet . . ." Our task, he insists, is to reconnect with that "deep masculinity" that lies within us.

There's some wisdom in what Bly says, but also a lot of blarney. There is indeed a residual memory of what we were meant to be, but it's not something we can capture and cage on our own.

No amount of Wild Man meetings, sweat lodge pow-wows, or scrumlike hugging will ever make us into real men. That's a job for God. It took God to make a man in the beginning—and it still does.

How God does it is the theme of this book—a book based on seventeen stories God tells in his book. Reading them allows us to look over his shoulder and watch him at work.

Over the last seventeen years I have gathered almost every Wednesday morning with a group of men to study the lives of biblical men and women. Our main purpose is to strengthen one another's grip on God. We are men from many backgrounds—Catholics and Protestants, charismatics and noncharismatics, long-time believers, novice Christians, cynics, skeptics, and seekers who are still on the way. It's a place where anyone can air his thoughts or doubts and be accepted. They really love a fellow there.

Out of our discussions have come a stream of ideas and insights that have informed my thinking and changed my life. This book, at least in part, represents the collective savvy of this group of men.

One thing I have learned is that God has many ways to make a man, but it seems that his preferred method is through resistance. The greater the resistance, the greater the growth. What we see as obstacles to achievement, God sees as opportunities for growth. Disappointment, loss, criticism, failure, humiliation, temptation, depression, loneliness, and moral failure become the means by which we grow strong if we are "trained" by these forces, as the author of Hebrews would say (12:11). That's what this book is mainly about. God wastes nothing—not even sin.

I've not tried to be gender-sensitive as I write, as important as that is to me in other contexts. This is unabashedly a book for men. I write as a man for men because I love men and I want to see them come into their own.

The Talmud says there are three things a man ought to do before he dies: plant a tree, have a child, and write a book, which means, I suppose, that he ought to leave something behind that endures—something that prolongs his usefulness. That's why I have written this book.

My usefulness, as I see it, lies partly in the degree to which I have helped other men become more godly and more manly than ever before. If this book does that for you I've accomplished my purpose in writing it.

Years ago I read an introduction to a commentary by Matthew Henry that states well my thoughts as I write: "If I may but be instrumental to make my readers wise and good, wiser and better . . . and more in love with God and His Word, I have all I desire, all I aim at."

Who could ask for anything more?

Joseph

IRON IN OUR SOULS

Life is not as idle ore,
but iron dug from central gloom,
*   And heated hot with burning fears,*
*   and dipped in baths of hissing tears,*
And battered by the shocks of doom
to shape and use.

—Alfred, Lord Tennyson

Schroeder, garbed in oversize catcher's mask and chest protector, strides out to the mound, hands Charlie Brown the ball, and says, "The bases are loaded again, and there's still nobody out."

"So what do you think?" Charlie Brown asks.

Schroeder ponders the question for a moment and replies: "We live in difficult times."

Indeed we do. As a friend of mine laments, "If it's not one thing it's another, and some days it's both." Painful, mortifying, and expensive things keep happening to us. "One woe doth tread upon another's heel so fast they follow," Hamlet complained—cruel events that seem devoid of sense and meaning, bitter ironies that thwart our desires, foil our plans, frustrate our hopes, and break our hearts.

13

And the beat goes on. We keep telling ourselves that things will get better and life will get easier as we get along in years, but that's a fool's dream. Sometimes the harder tests are farther along.

When Earl Weaver was manager of the Baltimore Orioles and bane of American League umpires, he used to charge out of the dugout bellowing, "Is it going to get any better or is this it?"

Well, I hate to tell you, but this is it! Things may not get better; they may get worse. It is the worst of all worlds. In fact it could not be any worse.

I used to think that life was mostly fun and games with a bit of trouble thrown in now and then to keep me honest; now I know it's the other way 'round: there are serendipities and other happy surprises along the way, but most of life is a vale of tears. The basis of life is tragedy.

And so I ask myself, Is there some reason to endure my troubles, some meaning for them beyond myself and my present circumstances?

When confronting these questions, which I must do from time to time, I think of Joseph, whose stress-filled and star-crossed life touches me to the core. Through his suffering, I have come to learn the meaning of my own.

Some years ago I came across the following psalm, one section of which amounts to a summary of Joseph's life story.

> He [God] called down famine on the land [of Canaan]
>   and destroyed all their supplies of food;
> and he sent a man before them—
>   Joseph, sold as a slave.
> They bruised his feet with shackles,
>   his neck [Hebrew: soul] was put in irons,
> till what he foretold came to pass,
>   till the word of the LORD proved him true.
> The king sent and released him,

the ruler of peoples set him free.
He made him master of his household,
    ruler over all he possessed,
to instruct his princes as he pleased
    and teach his elders wisdom (Psalm 105:16–22).

The Hebrew text of the last line of verse 18 reads curiously, "his soul came into iron," a phrase ancient Jewish translators and rabbinical exegetes interpreted to mean, "iron entered into his soul."

If this translation is correct, and I believe it is, it has to do with one of the ways by which God turns us into stronger and better men—He puts iron into our souls.

The preparation

Joseph was cursed from the beginning. He was his father's favorite son, an unhappy circumstance that earned him the deep dislike of his brothers.

But then Joseph cursed himself as well. He added to his brother's resentment by flaunting his most-favored status, literally wearing it on his sleeve. The "coat of many colors" he wore was actually a long-sleeved garment with stripes on the sleeves to indicate rank. The reason he wore it was to parade his own importance and put his brothers down.

Joseph further distanced himself from his family by endlessly relating a set of dreams about his future happiness—dreams that in fact turned out to be true, but which, when repeated again and again, only fueled the resentment of his brothers: they "hated him all the more because of his dreams and his *words*" (Genesis 37:8).

Joseph had a lot of growing up to do. Israel's wise men would have called him a *peti*—a young, untutored fool.

God's problem, if I can put it that way, was to prepare a place for his people. Jacob's sons had assimilated into

Canaanite culture, even the best of them, Judah, buying into the corrupt morality of the land (see Genesis 38). It was necessary to extrude the family from Canaan to cure them of its corruption. But before God could prepare a place for his people, he had to prepare a man for that place. And this is the story of that preparation.

"God's preparation," Oswald Chambers said, "is definite, drastic, and destructive." The making of Joseph was all of that. A series of shocking and calamitous events cascaded down on his head, like bricks tumbling out of a dump truck. He was snatched from his doting father by his brothers, cast into a pit and passed on to a band of Bedouins who in turn sold him into slavery in Egypt.

In Egypt, though we are told repeatedly that "God was with him" (Genesis 39:2–3, 21), his life unfolded into a series of tragic indignities. He was tempted by a determined seductress who, when spurned, accused him of raping her. He was summarily tried, convicted, imprisoned, and left to languish in companionless isolation for a dozen years or more, forgotten by family and friends. His life became a series of terrifying intrusions.

Like Roy Hobbs, the protagonist in the movie and the novel, *The Natural*, Joseph "never thought his life would end up like this." The pit and prison were things he'd never dreamed of.

And in your life and mine, are there not things we could never have foreseen: deep disappointment over what might have been; unrelieved heartache over dysfunctional families, unfaithful spouses and friends; piercing sorrow over lost loves; lonely dark periods that hide the face of God and obscure his Word?

The question is, How do we regard these intrusions? Have we grown bitter and resentful against them, against the people who forced them on us, against God? Are we frustrated because our plans have been disrupted? Are we full of bitterness and cynicism because we think some blind fury is against us?

There is a better way: the way God's humble saints have always gone. It is to know that Love and Wisdom is guiding all the way. God is working out his purpose in spite of all that happens to us. He is working though he does not seem to be working at all. Quietly, invisibly, inexorably he is taking the worst that is happening to us and slowly turning it into good.

Listen to Joseph when life's lessons were drawing to a close: "You sold me," he said to his brothers, "*but God sent me*" (Genesis 45:4–5). "You intended to harm me, *but God intended it for good to accomplish what is now being done, the saving of many lives*" (Genesis 50:20).

Behind every circumstance of his difficult life, Joseph saw the good intention and guiding hand of his Father, working through every circumstance to accomplish his will.

Missionary statesman Eric Liddell, best known as the hero of the movie *Chariots of Fire*, has written, "Circumstances may appear to wreck our lives and God's plans, but God is not helpless among the ruins. Our broken lives are not lost or useless. God's love is still working. He comes in and takes the calamity and uses it victoriously, working out his wonderful plan of love."

My friend and mentor Ray Stedman used to say that one mark of maturity is the capacity to ignore secondary causes. The main thing is to see God "working out his wonderful plan of love" in *everything* that comes our way. Whether our circumstances come from human beings or some devil, all creatures are under God's control. They are "holding to our lips the cup which the Father's hand has mixed" (F. B. Meyer).

God is not implicated in any way in the evil that others do, but he assumes control and accepts responsibility for everything that happens to us. When Satan appeared before God after doing his worst to destroy Job, the Lord said to him, "You incited *me* against [Job] to ruin him" (Job 2:3). There are no accidents in God's universe, no maverick molecules to spoil his plan. "His purpose is everywhere at work" (Ephesians 1:11 NEB). "What do you understand by the Providence of God?" the Heidelberg Catechism asks. "The almighty and ever-present power of God whereby He still upholds, as it were by His own hand, heaven and earth together with all creatures, and rules in such a way that leaves and grass, rain and drought, fruitful and unfruitful years, food and drink, health and sickness, riches and poverty, and everything else come to us not by chance but by His fatherly hand."

This is the mystery of Sovereignty: God works in spite of evil. No, he works *through* evil to accomplish his will. "He permits evil," Augustine said, "to transform it into greater good."

"Everything is against me!" Jacob cried in his distress (Genesis 42:36). No, "In all things God works for the good of those who love him, who have been called according to his purpose" (Romans 8:28).

Annie Johnson Flint, that arthritic poet who herself wrote "through nights devoid of ease," put it this way:

In a factory building there are wheels and gearings,
There are cranks and pulleys, beltings tight or slack,
Some are whirling swiftly, some are turning slowly,
Some are thrusting forward, some are pulling back;

Some are smooth and silent, some are rough and noisy,
Pounding, rattling, clanking, moving with a jerk;
In a wild confusion, in a seeming chaos,
Lifting, pushing, driving, but they do their work.

From the mightiest lever to the tiniest pinion,
All things move together for the purpose planned;

And behind the working is a mind controlling,
And a force directing, and a guiding hand.

So all things are working for the Lord's beloved;
Some things might be hurtful if alone they stood;
Some might seem to hinder, some might draw us backward;
But they work together, and they work for good;

All the thwarted longings, all the stern denials,
All the contradictions, hard to understand.
And the force that holds them, speeds them and retards them,
Stops and starts and guides them, is our Father's hand.

What God is about

Søren Kierkegaard, Danish philosopher and theologian, once pointed out that most of us are like the schoolboy who stole the teacher's answers before a math exam. Our aim is to memorize the answers so we won't have to work through the problems.

The problem with suffering, however, is that sometimes there's simply no answers, at least no earthly answers: now we "know in part"; we see only "the fringes of His ways" (Job 26:14 NASB). The full explanation awaits heaven where God will supply the reasons for all that we've been going through. In the meantime we have to rest in the fact that there is more to life than we can know. "A real Christian is an avowed agnostic," Oswald Chambers said. "His attitude is 'I have reached the limit of my knowledge. From here on I must trust God.' "

I write this because I'm always a little uneasy around those sincere but too-certain folks who can explain everything that comes my way. Like Job's comforters their answers, though well-meaning, only make me more miserable. I'm much more comfortable with those who say to me, "I'm not sure why you're suffering, but I'll wait here with you and pray." Friends like that are a pure benediction.

God is working for *our* good

It's said of Jesus that, "although he was a son, he learned obedience from what he suffered" (Hebrews 5:8). The worst brought out the best in our Lord; he was made perfect through misery and tears (Hebrews 2:10).

Why should we expect less? "To this you were called," Peter insists, "because Christ suffered for you, leaving you an example, that you should follow in his steps" (1 Peter 2:21).

Repeated rejection, deep loneliness, deferred hope are the means God used to shape his Son into the matchless man he became. Should we be surprised that he does the same for you and me?

Emerson wrote as though thinking of Joseph, "Chambers of the great are jails,/And head winds right for royal sails." God is making us *great*. He is shaping us into men whose lives are redolent with beauty and grace. Through suffering we learn to bear pain without complaint; to endure insult without retaliation; to suffer shame without bitterness. He makes us more like the men we have always wanted to be.

We learn to "live friendly," as Quakers say. We become more patient with others, more tolerant of their weaknesses and failures, kinder, gentler folk, easier to get along with, easier to work with, easier to be around.

We learn to deal with our discomfort and discontent with things as they are. We become more "peaceful, considerate, submissive, full of mercy and good fruit, impartial and sincere—peacemakers who sow in peace and raise a harvest of righteousness" (James 3:17–18).

"Sorrow is better than laughter," Solomon said, because it's "good for the heart" (Ecclesiastes 7:3). Sorrow—with bitterness removed—uncovers hidden depth in us. It makes us think long and earnestly about ourselves and the kind of men we are. It makes us ponder our behavior, our motives, our intentions, our real interests. We learn to know ourselves as never before.

Robert Browning Hamilton put it this way:

> *I walked a mile with Pleasure*
> *She chattered all the way;*
> *But left me none the wiser*
> *For all she had to say.*

> *I walked a mile with Sorrow,*
> *And ne'er a word said she;*
> *But, oh, the things I learned from her*
> *When Sorrow walked with me.*

Most of all, our suffering enables us to know God as we've never known him before. Job said of his own misery: "My ears had heard of you but now my eyes have *seen* you" (Job 42:5). In the words of an old Audrey Meier song, God washed Job's eyes with tears so he could see.

Sorrow is the means to that end to all things—God himself. It brings us heart to heart with him. Paul said he rejoiced in his sufferings because suffering produced perseverance, proven character, and hope (Romans 5:3). But more than that, he insisted, it taught him to "rejoice in God" (Romans 5:11).

When repeated strokes have robbed us of health, friends, money, and favorable circumstances, God then becomes the only thing in life for us. We come to love him for himself and not for what he has to give. We cry out with the psalmist, "Whom have I in heaven but you? And earth has nothing I desire besides you." The nearness of God becomes our only good (73:25–28).

"What do you think of your God now?" asked a cynic of an old saint, who for twenty years had suffered great physical pain. "I think of him more than ever," was the reply. This is the sweet aftermath of suffering.

When it comes down to it, I don't think God can do much with any of us until he has taught us to mourn.

God is working for others' good

Pain serves another purpose, one beyond ourselves: it is meant for others. It prepares us to connect with the deeper needs of those around us and to give comfort and counsel on a level we could never otherwise give.

Paul writes,

> Praise be to the God and Father of our Lord Jesus Christ, the Father of compassion and the God of all comfort, *who comforts us in all our troubles, so that we can comfort those in any trouble with the comfort we ourselves have received from God.* For just as the sufferings of Christ flow over into our lives, so also through Christ our comfort overflows. If we are distressed, it is for your comfort and salvation; if we are comforted, it is for your comfort, which produces in you patient endurance of the same sufferings we suffer (2 Corinthians 1:3–6).

God's messengers are sent to the weary. There are so many of these folks in the world. They need those who have been comforted with God's comfort and who can give that comfort to others. To do this requires months and sometimes years of lonely suffering.

Years ago I heard J. Oswald Sanders relate an incident that took place early in his ministry. He had spoken in a church and in his own estimate had hit the long ball. On the way out he overheard two elderly women critiquing his message: "What did you think of Mr. Sanders?" one asked. "Oh, he'll be much better," the other replied, "when he's suffered a little."

The needs of people around us are exceedingly profound. Hurt by the complexities and cruelties of life, they cry "out of the depths," as the psalmist did. Those who have known deep sorrow themselves can speak to that fathomless deep in others. They have great compassion for those who suffer; they can speak to the misery that others feel. In the words of an old ballad, "the anguish of the singer makes the purest, sweet refrain."

Oswald Chambers wrote this in *Baffled to Fight Better*:

> In his epistle Peter refers to those who have plenty of time for others. They are those who have been through suffering, but now seem full of joy. If a man has not been through suffering he will snub others unless they share his interests. He is no more concerned about them than the desert sand; but those who have been through things are not now taken up with their own sorrows. They have been made broken bread and poured out wine for others. You can always be sure of the man who has been through suffering, but never of the man who has not.

"You speak like one who has suffered," said Arctura, one of George MacDonald's characters. "That is how we are able to help others," was the reply. When it comes down to it, God uses best those who are closest to tears.

> Those who sow in tears
>   will reap with songs of joy.
> He who goes out weeping,
>   carrying seed to sow,
> will return with songs of joy,
>   carrying sheaves with him
> (Psalm 126:5–6).

Afterthoughts

There are other thoughts that come to mind as I think about my own pain. The first is that suffering does not last forever. There will be an end. The apostle Peter writes,

> In this you greatly rejoice, though now for *a little while* you may have had to suffer grief in all kinds of trials. These have come so that your faith—of greater worth than gold, which perishes even though refined by fire—may be proved genuine and may result in praise, glory and honor when Jesus Christ is revealed (1 Peter 1:6–7).

And again he says,

> After you have suffered *a little while,* [the God of all grace] will himself restore you and make you strong, firm and steadfast (1 Peter 5:10).

"God has come to wipe away our tears," George MacDonald wrote. "He is doing it; he will have it done as soon as he can; and until he can he would have them flow without bitterness; to which end he tells us it is a blessed thing to mourn because of the comfort that is on its way."

While we wait for that comfort, we can be assured that God mitigates our suffering. He will not allow us to be pushed beyond our ability to bear it. Every hour is timed with exact precision. Every situation is screened through his love. We will not suffer one moment more nor will we suffer more intensely than is necessary. "To a close-shorn sheep God gives wind by measure," is an old Basque saying.

Furthermore, for every moment of distress there is an ample supply of God's grace. It arrives with every ordeal. "Give us this day our *daily* bread" applies to every gift God gives. "As your days, so shall your strength be" (Deuteronomy 33:25). God has said,

> When you pass through the waters, I will be with you;
> and when you pass through the rivers, they will not
> sweep over you. When you walk through the fire, you
> will not be burned; the flames will not set you ablaze
> (Isaiah 43:2).

There will be deep waters through which we must wade; there will be fire through which the ore of our character must pass. But in the midst of them God promises to be our partner, our companion and faithful friend. He has called us into fellowship with him and he will see us through.

And then, when he has completed his work and we are fit for his kingdom, he will take us home. What a day that will be!

> Never again will we hunger;
>   never again will we thirst.
> The sun will not beat upon them,
>   nor any scorching heat.
> For the Lamb at the center of the throne will be their
>   shepherd;
>   he will lead them to springs of living water.
> And God will wipe away every tear from their eyes
> (Revelation 7:16).

Isaiah speaks of a day when "the former things will not be remembered, nor will they come to mind" (Isaiah 65:17). We cannot now forget the past, but some day our sad memories will fade away. We will not recall what once was intolerable—the sleepless nights, the humiliating failures, the final partings, the deep disappointments, the bitter death that broke off a life just as it was beginning to bloom. These are the "former things" that will be remembered no more. "When do we forget our sorrows?" Richard Baxter asks. "Is it not when we are home?"

Some years ago I read a story about an elderly couple returning from fifty years of stressful ministry as missionaries in Africa. As it turned out they were on a ship with the Beatles who were coming to America for their first visit.

When the ship reached New York there was a huge crowd awaiting the Beatle's arrival, but, due to an administrative mix-up, no one from the mission came to greet the couple. They were forced to retrieve their own trunks, load them in a taxi, locate an apartment, and move in by themselves. No one seemed to care.

Bitterness began to grow in the old gentleman, and he angrily complained to his wife, "We've come home and no one cares!" "Well now," she replied, "You must tell the Lord your trouble"—which he did. He went on a long walk and talked things over with God. When he returned, his wife knew by his face that his anger had dissipated.

"What happened?" she asked. He replied, "I got the first words out of my mouth, 'I've come home . . .' and the Lord interrupted me.

"What did he say?" his wife asked.

"Well," the old man replied, "He said, 'Ah, there's your problem. You've not yet come home.' "

Such a little while to wait! In the epistle to the Hebrews it is called "a very little while," literally, "yet a little while, how little, how little." It is a very little while when compared with the span of eternity; we will have endured a very light suffering when compared "with the glory that will be revealed in us" (Romans 8:18).

The noblest part

"Suffering is a great thing," Dostoevsky said. "You may not believe my words now, but you'll understand it someday." Ordinary men can never understand. These words can only be understood by those who know what God is about:

When God wants to drill a man
and thrill a man and skill a man
When God wants to mold a man
to play the noblest part;
When he yearns with all his heart
to create so bold a man
that all the world will be amazed,
Watch his methods, watch his ways:

How he relentlessly perfects
whom he royally elects;
How he hammers us and hurts us
and with mighty blows converts us
into trial shapes of clay
which only God can understand,
While our tortured heart is crying
and we lift beseeching hands.

How God bends, but never breaks
when his good he undertakes;
How he uses whom he chooses
and with every purpose fuses us;
By every act induces us
to try his splendor out—
God knows what he's about!

—Author unknown

Joseph was hammered and hurt more than anyone I know (except our Lord Jesus), but through it all he learned the meaning of his suffering and the measure of God's grace. When his sons were born he enshrined that lesson in their names:

He named his firstborn Manasseh and said, "It is because God has made me forget all my trouble and all my father's household." The second son he named Ephraim and said, "It is because God has made me *fruitful* in the land of my suffering" (Genesis 41:51–52).

Jacob said of Joseph in the end, "Joseph is a *fruitful* vine, a fruitful vine near a spring, whose branches climb over a wall" (Genesis 49:22).

> *My life is but a field*
> *stretched out beneath God's sky,*
> *Some harvest rich to yield.*
>
> *Where grows the golden grain?*
> *Where faith? Where sympathy?*
> *In a furrow cut by pain.*

—Maltbie Babcock

Gideon

THE STRENGTH
OF A MAN

So with the Lord He takes and He refuses;
Finds Him men whom others deny.
Neither strong ones nor mighty he chooses;
But such as John, or Gideon or I.

—F. B. Meyer

Some years ago I found myself in an elevator with a couple of other men. It was late at night and we all looked pretty wasted.

The elevator came to a stop and a larger-than-life Owyhee County buckaroo ambled in, wearing a battered Stetson, an old, stained sheepskin coat, and worn-out loggerboots. He looked around the elevator, met our eyes and growled, "Good evening, *men*." All of us straightened up. Trying to live up to the name.

"Living up to the name" is what men are mainly about. That's why we try to act macho. Yet for all our manly effort we know we never quite measure up. We're not the men we ought to be. Underneath the bragging and bravado we harbor a host of fears, inadequacies, and insecurities, a condition a friend of mine refers to as the "male chicken factor." Most of our manliness is pure bluff.

Paul was man enough to admit it: "We are weak" was his succinct point of view (1 Corinthians 14:10). That's not pious palaver. It's a humbling fact. Would that all of us were that truthful.

Weakness is the greatest experience of all. By an odd sort of irony, it is the means by which we become strong. Paul, who was inclined toward paradoxes, put it this way: "When I am weak, *then* I am strong" (2 Corinthians 12:10). It is awareness of our weakness that leads to strength.

Becoming strong

There is an imperative that occurs thirty times or more in the Bible: "Be strong and courageous." The verb translated "be strong" in almost every case means "play the man."

The Jewish scholars who first translated the Hebrew Bible into Greek almost always rendered that word with a corresponding Greek verb, *andridzomai*, which in classical sources meant "act like a man." It was an important word in a culture that literally idolized manliness.

The apostle Paul borrowed the verb and made significant use of it in 1 Corinthians 16:13, where he wrote, "Act like a man; be strong." The verb translated "act like a man" is based on the above-mentioned root, *andridzomai*. The verb translated "be strong" is actually passive and should be rendered, "be *made* strong." Paul understood well: the only way to be a man is to be *made* that way.

God fears our strength, and so should we. Strong men bluster about and get in God's way. There's little he can do with them. It's only the weak who can be made truly great. The strong can't be trusted with greatness.

That principle appears repeatedly in the Bible, but the story of Gideon may be the best example of all. Gideon was an ordinary man whom God made extraordinarily strong. More than that, he's a pattern for every man, and his life illustrates perfectly how God makes all of us strong.

The story begins in the book of Judges with Israel's domination at the hands of the Midianites:

> Again the Israelites did evil in the eyes of the LORD,
> and for seven years he gave them into the hands of the
> Midianites (6:1).

Two factors come to light: Israel's disobedience and the utter unfitness of anyone to deliver them from the results of their disobedience. No one could stem the tide.

The dominating power came from the east—the Midianites, the Amalekites, and various nomads from the Syrian desert. For seven years Israel endured the humiliation of periodic raids as waves of Bedouins swept across the countryside on camels, raping, pillaging, destroying what they could not carry away.

> Midian so impoverished the Israelites that they cried
> out to the LORD for help (6:6).

God heard their prayers—though offered as a last resort—and he sent help.

First God sent a prophet to tell his people where they had gone wrong. It's always God's way to be precise about our sin. The devil beats around the bush and fills our minds with vague, amorphous free-form guilt; not God: he puts his finger squarely on our sin:

> I said to you, "I am the LORD your God; do not
> worship the gods of the Amonites. . . ." But you have
> not listened to me (6:10).

The failure was theirs—not his. Nevertheless, God set out to bring salvation to his people. It is his way. We can never out-sin his love.

God in the hands of an angry man

> The angel of the LORD came and sat down under the
> oak in Ophrah that belonged to Joash the Abiezrite,
> where his son Gideon was threshing wheat in a
> winepress to keep it from the Midianites. When the
> angel of the LORD appeared to Gideon, he said, "The
> LORD is with you, mighty warrior."
>
> "But sir," Gideon replied, "if the LORD is with us,
> why has all this happened to us? Where are all his
> wonders that our fathers told us about when they said,
> 'Did not the LORD bring us up out of Egypt?' But now
> the LORD has abandoned us and put us into the hand of
> Midian."
>
> The LORD turned to him and said, "Go in the
> strength you have and save Israel out of Midian's
> hand. Am I not sending you?"
>
> "But Lord," Gideon asked, "how can I save Israel?
> My clan is the weakest in Manasseh, and I am the least
> in my family."
>
> The LORD answered, "I will be with you, and you
> will strike down all the Midianites together" (6:11–16).

The angel of the Lord—the Lord representing himself in
the form of an angel—appeared to Gideon who, at the time,
was hiding in a winepress, hunched down in a hollow in the
rocks, beating out wheat with a stick, improvising to save his
grain crop from the marauding Midianites.

God said to Gideon, "The LORD is with you, mighty
warrior," using an expression that denotes a member of the
military aristocracy.

Gideon missed the irony of the angel's greeting and
launched into a bitter diatribe:

> If the Lord is with us, why has all this happened to
> us? Where are all his wonders that our fathers told us

about when they said, 'Did not the Lord bring us up
out of Egypt?' But now the Lord has abandoned us
and put us into the hand of Midian (6:13).

"The Lord is with us?" "Where was he when the
Midianites burned my farm?" "Where was he when raiders
killed my two brothers?" (see Judges 8:18–21). "Where are
all these so-called 'wonders' that God has been telling us
about?"

What Gideon did not know was that God was already on
the move and that Gideon himself was the "wonder" that God
would work in the land.

The Lord shrugged off Gideon's assault and said to him,

"Go in the strength you have and save Israel out of
Midian's hand" (6:14).

Literally, "Go in this *your* strength." What strength?
Gideon had none! He was the "least" in his household (6:15).
The word means "trifling" or "small." Gideon was nobody.
Exactly! That was his strength.

"If I must boast," Paul wrote, "I will boast of the things
that show my weakness. The God and Father of the Lord
Jesus, who is to be praised for ever, knows that I am not
lying. In Damascus the governor under King Aretas had the
city of the Damascenes guarded in order to arrest me. But I
was lowered in a basket from a window in the wall and
slipped through his hands" (2 Corinthians 11:30–33).

Paul came to Damascus thinking he was God's gift to his
generation—perfectly suited to evangelize the Jews. He had
reason to be confident: "circumcised on the eighth day, of the
people of Israel, of the tribe of Benjamin, a Hebrew of
Hebrews; in regard to the law, a Pharisee; as for zeal,
persecuting the church; as for legalistic righteousness,
faultless" (Philippians 3:4–6). He was an Israelite indeed. He

was the little engine that could! And so he tackled the thing that couldn't be done, and he couldn't do it. Instead of a revival, he precipitated a riot.

The Christians in Damascus put him in a fish basket, lowered him over the wall and sent him away, pleading with him not to return lest he undo all that God had done.

What a bitter embarrassment! It was the worst day of Paul's life—*and the best*. That's the day he learned that he was, as he later put it, "nobody" (2 Corinthians 12:11).

But not to worry! Paul became "somebody." He rounds out the picture this way: "We have this treasure [Christ himself] in jars of clay [his body] to show that this all-surpassing power is from God and not from us" (2 Corinthians 4:7). Deity in humanity; God in a peanut-butter jar. Paul carried about in his weak and inadequate body the presence and essence of *God*.

We must accept our limits—no, we must *love* them. They are God's gift to us. It is the way we are. Nothing in us is a source of hope. Nothing in us is worth defending. Nothing in us is worth admiring. Every natural virtue, every endearing quality, every tendency toward goodness comes from God. Without him we can do nothing. When we accept that fact we can rest in him who alone is wisdom, righteousness, and power.

Our human reaction to any difficult assignment is to say, "I can't!" That's perfectly natural. But then God says, "My grace is sufficient for you; go in this your strength." At that moment, "I can't" becomes blasphemy.

God has promised to meet every need we have, but he cannot do it until we admit our need and cast ourselves on him. When we have done this, we don't have to worry about whether he will find us fit enough to do his work. In the words of the old hymn, "All the fitness he requireth is to feel our need of Him."

We should never say to God, "I can't do that" because we're too young or too inexperienced. Youth and inexperience are never a problem to God. Most of the biblical people God pressed into service were undeveloped: Jeremiah was a mere slip of a boy; the disciples were green and untested; even Jesus, from the standpoint of an old grizzly like me, was much too young to save the world. No, youthfulness never frustrates God. Only immaturity does, and immaturity can be outgrown by the grace of God.

Nor should we ever say no to God because we are afraid. We're *all* afraid. When President Franklin D. Roosevelt said, "The only thing we have to fear is fear itself," he was dead wrong. It's the absence of fear that we should fear.

Jacob and Wilhelm Grimm tell a fairy tale about a young man who was normal in every respect except that he could not shudder. All sorts of shocks were prepared for him—ghosts, hanged men, devil-cats, and bodies in coffins—but to no avail. He was hampered by his absence of fear.

Fear is the natural human reaction to any difficult or dangerous undertaking, and God does not condemn it. But he does not want us to be dominated by fear. Jesus' consistent word to his disciples was, "Don't be afraid," using a verb tense that suggests continuance: "Don't *keep on* fearing." We need not be intimidated by our fear or be overcome by it, for God can turn our fear into strength.

God calls us to get a grip on him and, by his power, walk through the walls of our fear. Courage is mastery of fear, not its absence. We should resist our fear—meet it with faith. Jesus has said, "I am with you always, to the very end of the age" (Matthew 28:20).

And so it comes to this: We should never worry about ourselves—our voice, our looks, our personalities, our education, our intelligence. God sets aside conventional notions of maturity, adequacy, and efficiency and looks for those who know their limitations. "This is the one I esteem," God assures us, "he who is humble and contrite in spirit, and trembles at my word" (Isaiah 66:2).

From weakness we are made strong. The realization that we are weak and powerless is the beginning of God's work.

We must "confess ourselves poor creatures," George MacDonald said, "for that is the beginning of being great. To try to persuade ourselves that we are something when we are nothing is terrible loss; to confess that we are nothing is to lay the foundation of being something."

This is the life: living without apparent power, prosperity, or adequacy, wholly dependent on God, available to him to be put to his intended use. We don't have to render the big answer. We don't have to perform the immortal deed. We don't have to be terrific or sensational. All we need is God.

And so it was for Gideon.

> The LORD answered, "I will be with you, and you will strike down all the Midianites together" (6:16).

Note the change in subject. When the angel of the Lord first appeared to Gideon, he said, "The LORD is with you." Now he says, "*I* will be with you"—and Gideon realizes to whom he is speaking. This is no messenger; this is God himself, putting in a personal appearance, assuring Gideon that he was Gideon's strength and success (6:17–24).

Courage begins at home

> That same night the LORD said to him, "Take the second bull from your father's herd, the one seven years old. Tear down your father's altar to Baal and cut down the Asherah pole beside it. Then build a proper kind of altar to the LORD your God on the top of this height. Using the wood of the Asherah pole that you cut down, offer the second bull as a burnt offering" (6:25–26).

Gideon's father was the custodian of a Baal sanctuary and probably its priest. For seven years he and his family had worshiped the sacred bulls. (The bull was the Canaanite symbol for the god Baal. Our English word *bull* is probably derived from the Semitic word *Baal*.) Now it was time for Gideon to pull that worship down.

Gideon was fearful—he worked under cover of darkness—but he got the job done. Courage is not the absence of fear. It is rather the capacity to draw on the resources of God to do what we know we must do—respond in obedience to his call and in total dependence on his power. "Courage is fear that has said its prayers," poet Karle Wilson Baker says.

Gideon acted despite his fear: he pulled down the altar to Baal, cut down the Asherah pole that stood beside it, built a proper altar on top of the fortress, where everyone could see it, and offered his father's sacred bull as a sacrifice to the living and true God.

The townsfolk were enraged, certain that Baal would now abandon them. They counted on Baal and his consort Asherah for rainfall and fertility. But Joash, Gideon's father, moved to faith by his son's obedience, flew to his defense: "If Baal is a god let him look after himself," he insisted. And then he dubbed his son "Jerubbaal"—"Baal fighter" became his nickname!

Courage begins at home. Perhaps the most difficult and dangerous task that you have to face lies within the four walls of your house: a spouse who does not love you, who is determined after years of marriage to "find herself" in someone or something other than you; a teenager in the midst of rebellion who has jettisoned all his or her family values and is in wild pursuit of satisfaction through sex and drugs. This is the place to begin.

Gideon did not shrink from the task. By God's grace he tackled the thing that "couldn't be done" and he did it. And so can you. There are no guarantees that your efforts will pay off as Gideon's did—at least not in this life. God gives men and women the right to choose, and they may choose against him and against their own best interests. Our task is not make everything right, but to be the right sort of men and leave the consequences to God. That's where his enablement comes in: he will provide what it takes to be the man he wants you to be right where you are.

The fabulous fleece

It was about that time that the Midianites, the Amalekites, and the people from the east conducted one of their annual raids and encamped in the valley of Jezreel (6:33). Then the Spirit of the Lord came upon Gideon, who mustered his clan, along with the three tribes of Israel located in that vicinity—Asher, Zebulun, and Naphtali (6:34–35).

Having gathered the tribes, Gideon had another failure of nerve—something that often happens on the eve of doing the thing we fear. Gideon asked for a sign that God was still with him. He said to God,

> "If you will save Israel by my hand as you have promised—look, I will place a wool fleece on the threshingfloor. If there is dew only on the fleece and all the ground is dry, then I will know that you will save Israel by my hand, as you said." And that is what happened. Gideon rose early the next day; he squeezed the fleece and wrung out the dew—a bowlful of water.
>
> Then Gideon said to God, "Do not be angry with me. Let me make just one more request. Allow me one more test with the fleece. This time make the fleece dry and the ground covered with dew." That night God did so. Only the fleece was dry; all the ground was covered with dew (6:36–40).

Gideon asked for something contrary to nature, but God met Gideon where he was, giving him the assurance he needed, for he knew that the demand on Gideon's faith was greater than he could bear.

Gideon is infamous for this incident. It's often cited as an example of putting God to the test, something we're told not to do. Or it's pointed out as an example of "little faith," a faith that needs signs and wonders to support it.

I suppose both suggestions are valid. Gideon was putting God to the test and Gideon didn't have a whole lot of faith at this point. But it was all the faith Gideon had, and God wanted to make it grow.

Faith is a growing thing. We grow "from faith to faith," as Paul said. We should pray as the disciples prayed, "Increase our faith!" Jesus said, "If you have faith as small as a mustard seed, you can say to this mulberry tree, 'Be uprooted and planted in the sea,' and it will obey you" (Luke 17:5–6).

Jesus' point is simply this: A little faith goes a long, long way. Exercising it is the way to make it grow.

The battle is joined

Israel encamped at the spring of Harod. The camp of Midian was north of them across the plain of Esdraelon near the hill of Moreh. The battle was about to be joined. Now was the time for God to ready his troops.

Confederate cavalry commander Nathan Bedford Forrest was once asked about his remarkable success at the battle of Murfreesboro. He explained, "I got there fustest with the mostest." Gideon's destiny was to get there with the "leastest," which is usually the way the Lord leads us into war.

Nebuchadnezzer, the archtypical worldling, said, I have accomplished great things "by my mighty power and for the glory of my majesty," relying on that humanistic trinity—me, myself, and I—making himself the measure of all things (Daniel 4:30). But we rely on another power: " 'Not by [your] might nor by [your] power, but by my Spirit,' says the LORD Almighty" (Zechariah 4:6).

The odds were stacked against Gideon's army 4 to 1. Midian had 135,000 foot soldiers (8:10); Gideon had 32,000 (7:3). The odds were all wrong, God told Gideon. "The people who are with you are too many for me" (7:2). So he decimated Gideon's army.

> Announce now to the people, "Anyone who trembles with fear may turn back and leave Mount Gilead." So twenty-two thousand men left, while ten thousand remained (7:3).

Now the odds were 13 to 1. God then further diminished Gideon's number:

> The LORD said to Gideon, "There are still too many men. Take them down to the water, and I will sift them out for you there. If I say, 'This one shall go with you,' he shall go; but if I say, 'This one shall not go with you,' he shall not go."
>
> So Gideon took the men down to the water. There the LORD told him, "Separate those who lap the water with their tongues like a dog from those who kneel down to drink." Three hundred men lapped with their hands to their mouths. All the rest got down on their knees to drink (7:4–6).

Now Gideon's army numbered 300. The odds were 450 to 1.

God not only dismembered Gideon's army, he disarmed them, taking away their swords and giving them trumpets and candles instead (7:16–18), turning them into a lean fighting machine. He did so because he wanted to make it clear that the battle belonged to the Lord!

Paul's says, "Though we live in the world, we do not wage war as the world does. The weapons we fight with are not the weapons of the world" (2 Corinthians 10:3–4). God's wars are never fought by numbers, though we incessantly crunch them. "Size is success," we say; the bigger the better. But not necessarily. God's way has usually been through small and insignificant beings.

Numbers, planning, formulae, techniques, and methods amount to nothing apart from God. It is by faith that the heroes of Hebrews conquered kingdoms, administered justice, gained what was promised, shut the mouths of lions, quenched the fury of flames, escaped the edge of the sword. It is by faith that "weakness was turned to strength; and [men and women] became powerful in battle and routed foreign armies" (Hebrews 11:33–34).

Blessed assurance

And so God, wanting to teach Gideon to operate on his strength, stripped him of every human resource. But knowing the state of his fledgling faith he gave him another assurance: "If you are afraid to attack, go down to the [enemy] camp with your servant Purah and listen to what they're saying" (7:10)

"*If* you are afraid!" Of course Gideon was afraid. And so he and his page made their way under cover of darkness to the outskirts of the camp where they heard two soldiers discussing a dream: one of them had seen a round barley loaf roll into camp and flatten their commander's tent.

Like most dreams, this one was murky and incongruous, but the soldiers interpreted it to mean defeat: "This can be nothing other than the sword of Gideon, son of Joash the Israelites. God has given the Midianites and the whole camp into his hands" (7:14).

Josephus, the Jewish historian, said that barley loaves were poor fare—tasteless, teeth-bending biscuits that were barely edible. The barley loaf was none other than Gideon.

The dream brought Gideon back to reality—back to "the simplicity and helplessness of his own resources according to F. B. Meyer:

In the gathering of these crowds of warriors, in the notoriety he had achieved, in the loyalty of the three hundred, there was much to inflate his pride. Therefore God had to bring him face to face with himself. He was only a cake of barley bread at the best. Before God can uplift, use, and anoint us, he must show us what we are, humbling and emptying us, bringing us into the dust of death. Before God can use thee to work a great deliverance, He must convince thee of being only a cake of barley bread. "Five barley loaves, and two small fishes."

A barley loaf is a small and worthless thing, but if God is the one who launches it, it can topple a tent, or a kingdom. Once it is set in motion by the Lord it has divine power to demolish strongholds! (2 Corinthians 10:4).

When Gideon heard the dream and its interpretation, he bowed behind his bush and worshiped. Then he returned to the camp of Israel and called out, "Get up! The LORD has given the Midianite camp into your hands" (7:15). Gideon now knew that victory was assured.

Gideon divided his rag-tag army into three units of one hundred each and stationed them on three sides of the Midianite camp. When he gave the signal, each soldier broke his pitcher, blew his trumpet and shouted at the top of his lungs: "A sword for the LORD and for Gideon." (Please note that there was no sword in anyone's hand.) And God routed the Midianites.

Panicked by the noise and lights and unable to see in the darkness, the Midianites believed they were being attacked by a superior force. They turned their swords on one another and decimated their own army. Then they fled to the east.

Not content with mere attack, Gideon chased the raiders into the desert and all the way back home, thus once for all putting an end to their domination (7:23–8:21).

The writer of Hebrews adds, "And what more shall I say? I do not have time to tell about Gideon, Barak, Samson, Jephthah, David, Samuel and the prophets, who through faith conquered kingdoms, administered justice, and gained what was promised; who shut the mouths of lions, quenched the fury of the flames, and escaped the edge of the sword; *whose weakness was turned to strength*; and who became powerful in battle and routed foreign armies" (Hebrews 11:32–34).

The agony of defeat

He was greatly helped until he became strong
(2 Chronicles 26:15).

After the battle, "the Israelites said to Gideon, 'Rule over us—you, your son and your grandson—because you saved us from the hand of Midian," but Gideon declined, adding piously, "The Lord himself will reign over you."

Though he would not accept the responsibility of leadership, he readily acceded to its perquisites. He lived a decidedly royal lifestyle, with many sons and daughters and wives and a mistress or two, one of which fathered a son whose name was a dead giveaway: "Abimelech," which means, "My father is a *king!*"

In the end he squandered away his life. Where did Gideon go wrong? He got to be too strong.

> *I only ask one thing of Thee;*
> *Give Thou Thyself and all is given*
> *I am not strong nor brave nor wise;*
> *Be Thou with me—it shall suffice.*

—Annie Johnson Flint

Manasseh

A FRESH AND
BETTER START

Some rise by sin, and some by virtue fall.

—Shakespeare

It was New Years Day, 1929. The University of California at Berkeley was playing Georgia Tech in the Rose Bowl. Roy Riegels, a Cal defensive back recovered a Georgia Tech fumble, ran laterally across the field, turned and scampered sixty-five yards in the wrong direction—straight toward Cal's goal line.

One of his own players, Benny Lomm, tackled Riegles just before he scored for Georgia Tech. On the next play Georgia Tech blocked the punt and scored.

From that day on Riegles was saddled with infamy: "Wrong-way Riegles was his name. For years afterward, whenever he was introduced, people would exclaim, "Oh, yeah. I know who you are! You're the guy who ran the wrong way in the Rose Bowl!"

It may be that our failures are not as conspicuous as Riegles, but we have our own alternate routes and wrong-way runs and we have the memories that accompany them—recollections that rise up to taunt us and haunt us at three o'clock in the morning. There's so much of our past we wish we could undo or redo—so much we wish we could forget. If only we could begin again.

Louis Fletcher Tarkington wrote for all of us when she mused,

> *I wish that there were some wonderful place*
> *Called the Land of Beginning Again,*
> *Where all our mistakes and all our heartaches*
> *And all of our poor selfish grief*
> *Could be dropped like a shabby old coat at the door*
> *And never put on again.*

There is such a place. It is found in the grace of God—a grace that not only completely forgives our past and puts it away, but uses it to make us better than ever before. "Even from sin," Augustine said, "God can draw good."

The prodigal king

There was a man named Manasseh . . .

> [He] was twelve years old when he became king, and he reigned fifty five years in Jerusalem; and his mother's name was Hephzibah (2 Kings 21:1).

Manasseh was the son of Hezekiah, one of the few kings of Judah who "did what was right in the eyes of the LORD" (2 Kings 18:3). Israel's historian tells us that Hezekiah

> removed the high places, smashed the sacred stones and cut down the Asherah poles. He broke into pieces the bronze snake Moses had made, for up to that time the

Israelites had been burning incense to it. (It was called Nehushtan.)

Hezekiah trusted in the LORD, the God of Israel. There was no one like him among all the kings of Judah, either before him or after him. He held fast to the LORD and did not cease to follow him; he kept the commands the LORD had given Moses (2 Kings 18:4–6).

Hezekiah was responsible for a historic spiritual revival that rejuvenated Judah. He did away with the idols that his father, Ahaz, had worshiped, and he delivered his people from apostasy. He was helped greatly in his work of reformation by the prophetic ministries of Isaiah and Micah.

There were at least two invasions of Judah during this time by Sennacherib, the king of Assyria. On both of these occasions the Lord miraculously protected Jerusalem. Although almost all of the land of Judah was devastated by the Assyrians, the capital city was preserved.

Sennacherib, in his annals said, "I shut up Hezekiah like a bird in a cage." Isaiah used a different metaphor: "The Daughter of Zion is left like a shelter in a vineyard, like a hut in a field of melons, like a city under siege" (Isaiah 1:8).

But God miraculously intervened:

That night [the night of the final siege] the angel of the LORD went out and put to death a hundred and eighty-five thousand men in the Assyrian camp. When the people got up the next morning—there were all the dead bodies! (2 Kings 19:35).

This was the spiritual climate in which Manasseh grew up.

Manasseh's dirty deeds

Manasseh ascended to the throne when he was twelve years old and reigned for ten years as co-regent with his father. When Manasseh was twenty-two, his father died and the young king took over the reins of government. He reigned from 692–638 B.C.—fifty-five years—the longest rule in the history of both Judah and Israel.

Manasseh had a godly father, lived through a time of spiritual vitality and prosperity, and was tutored by the prophets Isaiah and Micah. He saw firsthand the Lord deliver Jerusalem under siege by the Assyrians. And yet "he did evil in the eyes of the LORD, following the detestable practices of the nations the LORD had driven out before the Israelites" (2 Kings 21:2).

The "nations" of whom the author writes were the depraved and disgusting Canaanites. Manasseh outdid them in his insane frenzy to break every rule—a madness spelled out in the following verses:

> He rebuilt the high places his father Hezekiah had destroyed; he also erected altars to Baal and made an Asherah pole, as Ahab king of Israel had done. He bowed down to all the starry hosts and worshiped them. He built altars in the temple of the LORD, of which the LORD had said, "In Jerusalem I will put my Name."
>
> In both courts of the temple of the LORD, he built altars to all the starry hosts. He sacrificed his own son in the fire, practiced sorcery and divination, and consulted mediums and spiritists. He did much evil in the eyes of the LORD, provoking him to anger.
>
> He took the carved Asherah pole he had made and put it in the temple, of which the LORD had said to David and to his son Solomon, "In this temple and in Jerusalem, which I have chosen out of all the tribes of Israel, I will put my Name forever. I will not again make the feet of the Israelites wander from the land I gave their forefathers, if only they will be careful to do everything I commanded them and will keep the whole Law that my servant Moses gave them."

But the people did not listen. Manasseh led them astray, so that they did more evil than the nations the LORD had destroyed before the Israelites (2 Kings 21:3–9).

Manasseh's sins are recited here in an ascending order of deviance. First he "rebuilt the high places his father Hezekiah had destroyed." Ahaz, Manasseh's grandfather, had established "high places"—groves on the top of hills—where the Asherah was worshiped. Hezekiah had torn them down (2 Kings 18:4); Manasseh built them up again.

Then Manasseh "erected altars to Baal," the chief Canaanite deity, and he made an Asherah pole, as Ahab and Jezebel, Israel's diabolical duo had done (1 Kings 16:33). The Asherah were images of a female deity, the consort of Baal and represented the Canaanite goddess of sex and fertility. The pillars erected in her honor were evidently some sort of phallic symbols.

Manasseh worshiped the hosts of heaven and served them, giving his devotion to the sun, the moon, the planets, and the stars, and practicing astrology (see also Jeremiah 8:2; 19:13). He built altars to astral deities in the temple in Jerusalem, where God had said, "I will put My name."

He made his son pass through the fire—a child sacrifice. He slaughtered more than one of his sons. According to the chronicler, he sacrificed several "in the fire in the Valley of Ben Hinnom" (2 Chronicles 33:6).

He practiced augury, necromancy, witchcraft, and divination, and he "consulted mediums and spiritists." The Hebrew text suggests that he did more than consult them, he "appointed" them. In other words, he gave them court appointments, put them in his cabinet.

If this were not enough, this debauched monarch then "took the carved Asherah pole he had made and put it in the temple." He took the aforementioned pornographic post, dedicated to everything ugly and obscene, and set it up in the Holy of Holies in the Lord's temple.

Nowhere is there the slightest hint of the worship of Yahweh. Manasseh selected his pantheon from the cultures surrounding Israel—from the Amorites, the Canaanites, the Philistines, the Phoenicians—but there is not one reference to the God who had revealed himself to Israel.

The historian concludes: "Manasseh led [Israel] astray, so that they did more evil than the nations the LORD had destroyed before the Israelites" (2 Kings 21:9).

The descent of man

Sin always overtakes us and overwhelms us in the end. Though we think we're in control, sin eventually, inevitably dominates us and hurls us headlong into corruption and decay. Life becomes a steep downhill slide. "Everyone who sins is a slave to sin" (John 8:34).

Most of the time we're not even conscious of sin's control. That's because it overwhelms us so slowly and with such subtlety. Hosea said that Israel's sin "sapped his strength, but he did not realize it; his hair was sprinkled with gray, but he did not notice (Hosea 7:9).

That's the deceitfulness of sin: gradually and unconsciously we drift away from God. We lose control of our thoughts. The current carries us inexorably on until we are enslaved at last by greed and lust, our pathetic, feeble state evident to all eyes but our own. Sin has sapped our strength, but we do not know it.

> *It is strange: but life's currents drift us*
> *So surely and swiftly on*
> *That we scarcely note the changes*
> *And how many things are gone.*

—F. B. Meyer

So it was with Manasseh.

Yahweh's appeal

> The LORD said through his servants the prophets:
> "Manasseh king of Judah has committed these
> detestable sins. He has done more evil than the
> Amorites who preceded him and has led Judah into sin
> with his idols. Therefore this is what the LORD, the
> God of Israel, says: I am going to bring such disaster
> on Jerusalem and Judah that the ears of everyone who
> hears of it will tingle. I will stretch out over Jerusalem
> the measuring line used against Samaria and the
> plumbline used against the house of Ahab. I will wipe
> out Jerusalem as one wipes out a dish, wiping it and
> turning it upsidedown. I will forsake the remnant of
> my inheritance and hand them over to their enemies.
> They will be looted and plundered by all their foes,
> because they have done evil in my eyes and have
> provoked me to anger from the day their forefathers
> came out of Egypt until this day' (2 Kings 21:10–15).

The Amorites, to whom Manasseh is compared, were a
Canaanite subculture, notorious for their kinky practices. One
old Babylonian text reads, "The Amorite says to his wife,
'You be the man and I will be the woman.' "

The comparison suggests an uncurbed, lecherous lifestyle,
one that corrupted Manasseh and eventually eroded away the
moral fiber of his nation. "*He* led Judah into sin." He alone
was responsible.

Understand what's being said here: Manasseh alone bore
the responsibility for bringing an entire nation down. What a
legacy to leave behind!

And there is a final footnote, terrible in its implications . . .

> Manasseh also shed so much innocent blood that he filled
> Jerusalem from end to end—besides the sin that he had
> caused Judah to commit, so that they did evil in the eyes
> of the LORD (2 Kings 21:16).

Manasseh silenced the prophets with terrifying fury. Josephus, the Jewish historian, reports that Manasseh "slew all the righteous men that were among the Hebrews, nor would he spare the prophets, for he every day slew some of them until Jerusalem was overflown with blood."

There is a long-standing Jewish tradition reported in the Talmud that Manasseh put his old teacher, Isaiah, in a log and sawed it in two. This is almost certainly the background of the statement in the book of Hebrews that at least one of God's heroes was "sawn in two" (Hebrews 11:37).

What of Manasseh?

As for the other events of Manasseh's reign, and all he did, including the sin he committed, are they not written in the book of the annals of the kings of Judah? Manasseh rested with his fathers and was buried in his palace garden, the garden of Uzza. And Amon his son succeeded him as king (2 Kings 21:17–18).

Here is an odd thing: Manasseh thumbed his nose at God for fifty-five years, indulged himself in every lustful passion, corrupted and ruined an entire nation, and God sat on his hands.

Or did he?

> There is a line, by us unseen,
> That crosses every path;
> The hidden boundary between
> God's patience and His wrath.

—Joseph Addison Alexander

Normally, we see only one side of God—his long-suffering patience: "He is waiting to be gracious" (Isaiah 30:18). But there is another side: his "strange work" of judgment. Jeremy

Taylor says, "God threatens us with terrible things if we will not be happy."

The whole story is not told in the book of Kings. The purpose of 1 and 2 Kings is to trace the decline of Israel and Judah to the Babylonian exile and to supply the reasons for that exile. The stories are necessarily abridged. The writer dwells only on those facts that contribute to his theme.

The account of Manasseh's reign is resumed and supplemented in 2 Chronicles 33. The purpose of the Chronicler was different: his theme was the restoration of the Davidic throne and for this purpose he selected events that contributed to that motif. He included a number of facts that are omitted in Kings.

The first nine verses of 2 Chronicles 33 are basically a rewrite of 2 Kings 21:1–9 with a few minor changes. Then a new story emerges.

> The LORD spoke to Manasseh and his people, but they paid no attention (2 Chronicles 33:10).

God's judgment did not fall precipitously; it never does. Theologian John Piper says, "[God's] anger must be released by a stiff safety lock, but his mercy has a hair trigger."

God loves us too much to let us go. He pursues us—even into our sin and guilt—and pleads with us to turn back. An old Turkish proverb says that God has "feet of wool and hands of steel." We may not hear him coming, but when he gets his hands on us, we cannot wriggle away.

The flip side of the promise "I will never leave you nor forsake you" (Joshua 1:5) is the pledge that he will never leave us alone. He will hound us, badger us, bother us, pester us, heckle us until we give in.

George MacDonald says, "It's a terrible thing to be bad. All God's efforts are bent to deliver us from it, nor will he stop until we have given up being bad. God will have us good."

God has many ways to deliver us from sin. Sometimes by a drawing we feel in our souls; sometimes by a word dropped by a friend; sometimes by an incident related; or it by a book, a sermon, a chance meeting. In this way God appeals to us to come back to him.

I think of a student I met at Stanford University years ago, sitting on a bench in front of Memorial Church, reading a *Stanford Daily*. I sat down next to him, and we began to talk. The conversation went well until it turned to the subject of his relationship with God.

He leaped to his feet with a curse and stalked away. Then he stopped and turned around. "Forgive me," he said, "I was raised in a Christian home. My parents are Presbyterian missionaries in Taiwan, but I've been running away from God all my life. Yet wherever I go someone wants to talk to me about about God." As Francis Thompson learned, God's "strong feet" were following after, "with unhurrying chase and unperturbed pace."

More than anything our Lord wants us to give in to his love. "Love surrounds us," MacDonald said, "seeking the smallest crack by which it may enter in." God waits tirelessly, loves relentlessly. But if we will not have him, he will let us have our way and let us reap the consequences of our resistance. But even this is for our good. It is the *redemptive* judgment of God. God knows when the cold wind blows it may turn our head around.

> So the LORD brought against them the army
> commanders of the king of Assyria, who took
> Manasseh prisoner, put a hook in his nose, bound him
> with bronze shackles and took him to Babylon. In his
> distress he sought the favor of the LORD his God and
> humbled himself greatly before the God of his fathers.
> And when he prayed to him, the LORD was moved by
> his entreaty and listened to his plea; so he brought him

back to Jerusalem and to his kingdom. Then Manasseh knew that the LORD is God (2 Chronicles 33:11–12).

The Assyrian king mentioned here was probably Esar-haddon, the son of Sennacherib. Sennacherib died in 680 B.C., a date that corresponds to the traditional date of Isaiah's martyrdom. Manasseh's murder of God's prophet was evidently the last straw.

Sennacherib was succeeded by Esar-haddon. With the change of guard Manasseh, in concert with the king of Ethiopia, Tirhaka, led an insurrection against Assyria that swept up most of the other Assyrian provinces in the west.

Esar-haddon retaliated quickly, invading Judah and conquering Jerusalem. In his great prism, now displayed in the London Museum, Esar-haddon reports that he conquered twenty-two kings "on the other side of the river [Euphrates]" and that among them was "Me-na-si-i [Manasseh], king of Ia-ú-di [Judah]."

Esar-haddon put a ring in Manasseh's nose, manacles on his hands and feet and marched him off to Babylon where for twelve years he languished in a dungeon.

A ring in the nose was the Assyrian way of humiliating conquered kings, a custom clearly illustrated on Assyrian artifacts. One such carving depicts two conquered kings, portrayed as dwarfs beside the gigantic figure of Esar-haddon. He holds a rope that leads to rings in the noses of the smaller figures. The taller of the two small images is thought to be Tirhaka, king of Ethiopia, the more diminutive figure is Manasseh.

What utter humiliation! What awful ruin! But all to bring Manasseh home to God.

> *Well mayest thou then work on indocile hearts;*
> *By small successes, disappointments small;*
> *By nature, weather, failure or sore fall;*

By shame, anxiety, bitterness and smarts;
By loneliness, by weary loss of zest.
The rags, the husks, the swine, the hunger quest,
Drive home the wanderer to the Father's breast.

—George MacDonald

The way back

Recovery begins with shame. "To be ashamed is a holy and blessed thing," MacDonald said. "Shame is shame only to those who want to *appear*, not those who want to *be*. Shame is shame only to those who want to pass their examination, not to those who would get to the heart of things. . . . To be humbly ashamed is to be plunged in the cleansing bath of truth." Humility and contrition are the keys to the heart of God.

Those are the keys Manasseh used.

In his distress he sought the favor of the LORD his God and humbled himself greatly before the God of his fathers (2 Chronicles 33:12).

Josephus said that Manasseh "esteemed *himself* to be the cause of it all. He accepted full responsibility for what he had done—no denial, no excuses, no justification, no special pleading, no blame-shifting. Then Manasseh "humbled himself greatly."

Our tendency to make excuses for ourselves comes from thinking that God will never take us back unless we can minimize or explain away our wrongdoing. But, as C. S. Lewis observed, "Real forgiveness means looking steadily at the sin, that sin that is left over without any excuse, after all allowances have been made, and seeing it in all its horror, dirt, meanness, and malice, and nevertheless being wholly reconciled to the one who has done it. That, and only that, is forgiveness; and that we can always have from [God]."

Manasseh was not forsaken. Despite his monstrous wickedness, the Lord was still Manasseh's God. Though anger swept across God's face, he never turned away his eyes.

Inexorable love

Harriet Beecher Stowe's Uncle Tom laments, "I's wicked I is; mighty wicked; anyhow I can't help it!"

Sin is our usual thing. It is how we make our way through life—and we can't help it. Yet our repeated failures do not change God's fundamental disposition toward us. If it's our nature to sin, it's his nature to save. Without that understanding we could never survive our sin. It would only terrorize us and drive us away from God.

We'd have grounds for that terror if God had chosen us in the beginning because we were so wonderful. But since our original acceptance did not depend on anything in us, it cannot be undone by anything in us now. Nothing in us deserved his favor before our conversion; nothing in us merits its continuation.

God saved us because he determined to do so. He created us for himself and without that fellowship his heart aches in loneliness. That's why Christ suffered for us—"the righteous for the unrighteous, to bring [us] to God" (1 Peter 3:18). He will *never* give up. He loves us too much to give up. "He who began a good work in [us] will carry it on to completion" (Philippians 1:6).

Bernard of Clairvaux, the twelfth-century saint, wrote this of God's generous forgiveness:

No sinful man should ever despair—even if he has sinned ever so greatly, or ever so often, or ever so long. We have an example in Peter who denied Christ; in Paul who pursued the Church; in Matthew and Zaccheus who were publicans; in Mary Magdalene

who was a sinful woman; in the woman who was
taken in adultery; in the thief who hung on the cross
beside Christ; in Mary the Egyptian; and in
innumerable other grievous and great sinners.

We must accept God's full and free forgiveness and then
forget ourselves. That we are sinners is undeniably true. That
we are *forgiven* sinners is undeniable as well. We must not
dwell on our sinfulness. God's heart is open to us. We must
take what forgiveness we need and get on with the business of
living.

"We remain such creeping Christians," said George
MacDonald, "because we gaze at the marks of our own soiled
feet, and the trail of our own defiled garments. . . . We mourn
over the defilement to ourselves, and the shame of it before
our friends, children or servants, instead of hastening to make
the due confession and then forget our own paltry self with its
well-earned disgrace and lift up our eyes to the glory which
alone will quicken us."

Better than ever

There is more. God not only forgives our sin, he uses it to
make us better than ever before. Consider Manasseh. He was
released from prison after twelve years and restored to his
throne at which time he set out to strengthen his defenses.

And when [Manasseh] prayed to him, the LORD was
moved by his entreaty and listened to his plea; so he
brought him back to Jerusalem and to his kingdom. Then
Manasseh knew that the LORD is God. He rebuilt the outer
wall of the City of David, west of the Gihon spring in the
valley, as far as the entrance of the Fish Gate and
encircling the hill of Ophel; he also made it much higher.
He stationed military commanders in all the fortified cities

in Judah. He got rid of the foreign gods and removed the image from the temple of the LORD, as well as all the altars he had built on the temple hill and in Jerusalem; and he threw them out of the city. Then he restored the altar of the LORD and sacrificed fellowship offerings and thank-offerings on it, and told Judah to serve the LORD, the God of Israel (2 Chronicles 33:13–17).

Manasseh destroyed his pagan gods and removed the terrible idol he had set up in the house of the Lord. He hated his idols with as much fervor as he had loved them before.

He repaired the altar of the Lord, which he had broken down. He sacrificed on it peace-offerings and thank-offerings to praise God for his deliverance. He used his power now to reform his people rather than to corrupt them.

This is what John the Baptist described as "fruit in keeping with repentance" (Matthew 3:8). True repentance involves a fundamental change in our outlook and attitude. It is not mere sorrow over sin. It is a radical reversal of our thinking. It will manifest itself in a determined effort to strengthen ourselves in those areas where we are weak and where we have fallen before. There will be a fierce determination to guard ourselves against sin.

True repentance will mean staying away from the company of a man or woman whose influence corrupts us. It will mean staying out of situations in which we're inclined to stumble and fall. It will mean staying away from polluting influences in movies, books, magazines, and cyberspace. It will mean finding another man to hold us accountable when we travel, someone who will keep us honest when we're away from home. Whatever it means, our waywardness will have made us stronger and better than ever before. Even from our sin God has drawn good.

God gave Manasseh twenty more years of rule. He got a fresh and better start, and he made the most of it. He became one of the greatest kings of Judah, and for twenty-two years was a glorious example to Israel of God's unimaginable grace. God will do the same for you.

What's in a name?

Manasseh's name is taken from a Hebrew verb that means "to forget." That's the word God writes over Manasseh's past and ours—*forgotten.* "I will forgive [your] wickedness and will remember [your] sins no more" (Jeremiah 31:34). Oswald Chambers says, "God forgets away our sins."

Jeffrey Dahmer comes to mind when sin of unforgivable proportion is considered. Dahmer confessed to murdering seventeen young men, dismembering some, having sex with their corpses, and eating parts of their bodies.

The media exposure surrounding his crimes turned Dahmer into a national symbol of evil. After his bloody death, at the Columbia Correctional Center in Wisconsin, everyone was convinced that Dahmer was going straight to hell. One columnist uttered a fervent plea to the powers of darkness: "Take Jeffrey Dahmer, please."

But as it turned out, Dahmer had begun attending Bible studies in prison. He subsequently made a public profession of faith in Jesus Christ and was baptized. He found forgiveness and peace. He was calm about his fate, even after an inmate attempted to slit his throat during a chapel service. If he was sincere, and it appears that he was, we will see him one day in heaven.

Odd, isn't it? But such is the grace of God.

Postscript

During half-time of that Rose Bowl game in 1929, Riegles hid in a corner of the UCLA locker room with a towel over his head. His coach, Nibbs Price, said nothing to him and very little to the team.

Three minutes before the second half he said quietly, "The team that started the first half will start the second half. Riegles called out: "I can't, coach; I can't go back in. I've humiliated the team, the school, myself. I can't go back in." "Get back in the game, Riegles," Price replied, "it's only half over."

What a coach! What a God!

Elijah

DARK NIGHT OF THE SOUL

The great world's altar stairs
That slope through darkness up to God.

—Alfred, Lord Tennyson

St. John of the Cross wrote,

God perceives the imperfections within us, and because of his love for us, urges us to grow up. His love is not content to leave us in our weakness, and for this reason he takes us into a dark night. He weans us from all of the pleasures by giving us dry times and inward darkness. In doing so he is able to take away all these vices and create virtues within us. Through the dark night pride becomes humility, greed becomes simplicity, wrath becomes contentment, luxury becomes peace, gluttony becomes moderation, envy becomes joy, and sloth becomes strength. No soul will ever grow deep in the spiritual life unless God works passively in that soul by means of the Dark Night.

One of the best biblical examples of St. John's Dark Night is Elijah. Here's a man who stepped directly from the wondrous heights of Carmel into a dark, bleak canyon of despair. Israel's historian tells the story:

> Now Ahab told Jezebel everything Elijah had done and how he had killed all the prophets with the sword. So Jezebel sent a messenger to Elijah to say, "May the gods deal with me, be it ever so severely, if by this time tomorrow I do not make your life like that of one of them." Elijah was afraid and ran for his life. When he came to Beersheba in Judah, he left his servant there, while he himself went a day's journey into the desert. He came to a broom tree, sat down under it and prayed that he might die. "I have had enough, LORD," he said. "Take my life; I am no better than my ancestors." Then he lay down under the tree and fell asleep (1 Kings 19:1–5).

Exhilarated by his success on Mt. Carmel, the prophet "outran Ahab to Jezreel," a distance of about twenty-five miles. As Elijah ran, illusions of grandeur danced in his head: the death of state Baalism, a court chaplaincy, legislative prayer breakfasts, another opportunity to vindicate God's honor and make His mark on the world.

But Jezebel had another idea: "Dream on," she said and sent a messenger with this bit of terse verse: "May the gods deal with me, be it ever so severely, if by this time tomorrow I do not make your life like that of one of them" (19:2). Elijah's snappy rejoinder was to turn and flee: "Elijah was afraid and ran for his life" (19:3). The text may also be translated, "Elijah *saw!*" He got the picture!

Fueled by raw fear, Elijah ran all the way to Beersheba, a distance of about seventy miles, where he found shelter under a broom tree, dropped from exhaustion and prayed that he might die. "I have had enough, Lord," he said. "Take my life; I am no better than my ancestors" (19:4). "Enough!" he cried. "I'm a failure! I quit!"

Elijah's come-down is classic. Over-extended and emotionally depleted, brooding over his feelings of inadequacy and apparent failure, he collapsed into self-pity, withdrawal, and self-destructive thoughts.

Everyone has times of deep discouragement. Time and pain wear down our resolve. Broken in spirit and bruised beyond repair, we get weary of soul.

We ask ourselves, "What have I been spending my life for? Who is any better off from all my effort?" We find no pleasure or consolation in God or in his work.

There is an abiding sense of failure. Our yoke seems unbearable; our burdens are heavy beyond endurance. And what makes our difficulties even more grievous is that we feel such terrible loneliness: no one seems to care; no one shares our outlook; even God seems to be shunning us. And so, like Elijah, we cry, "Enough already!"

Sometimes our dark moods are nothing more than physical and emotional depletion. Like Elijah we've been running scared, over-doing everything, committing ourselves to more projects and plans than anyone could ever do. We string ourselves out, expending all our time and energy trying to be all things to all people at all times, adding our will to God's, trying to do well what he never intended for us to do at all.

We tax our bodies and give them no chance to recover. We provide no margins in which to adjust to unexpected emergencies. Over-worked and under-slept, we finally reach our yield point and fold. Our bodies can't take it anymore. Unlike that battery-powered bunny we just can't keep going.

It's good to know that our melancholy may be nothing but natural weariness. We're too inclined to make something spiritual out of it, thinking that somehow we've gone wrong. We've forgotten that we're only human, that "we have this treasure [Christ's divinity] in vessels of common clay [our humanity]" (2 Corinthians 4:7). The treasure is the only enduring element; the rest of us is frail and gives way easily.

"Fatigue makes cowards of us all," Vince Lombardi said. We start to lose focus and lose our grasp on reality. We implode—withdraw into a state of self-condemnation and apathy. We lose focus and concentration. We say things that we would never say if we were fresh and well-rested. We make unwise decisions based on feelings of inadequacy, and sometimes the decisions are irreversible. We should never trivialize our weariness.

> Elijah lay down under the tree and fell asleep. All at once an angel touched him and said, "Get up and eat." He looked around, and there by his head was a cake of bread baked over hot coals, and a jar of water. He ate and drank and then lay down again. The angel of the LORD came back a second time and touched him and said, "get up and eat, for the journey is too much for you." So he got up and ate and drank (19:5–8).

God understood Elijah's weary despair, and he let him sleep. Sleep is God's gift to his weary servants: "He grants sleep to those he loves" (Psalm 127:2). Sometimes the most urgent and vital thing you can do is to take a complete rest. Being spiritual doesn't necessarily mean expending effort in contemplation and prayer; it may mean eating supper and hitting the sack.

God sent his angel to touch Elijah. No lecture, no rebuke, no chiding—only a gentle touch from one of the Lord's tender angels, awakening Elijah to find food and drink. He commands his angels concerning us, to keep us in all our ways (Psalm 91:11).

God finds us when we're down and out, when we have nothing left to give. He comes to take away our weariness. He never awakens anyone to disappointment, but to the good things Love has prepared.

John, who learned God's love on Jesus' breast, tells in words so simple and direct: "We know and rely on the love God has for us" (1 John 4:16). I go back to these words again and again.

Perhaps the best way to know God's love is to experience it in times of declension and deep discouragement, when we feel most undeserving of it. "His lovingkindness is better than life" (Psalm 63:3).

Strengthened by food and rest Elijah "traveled forty days and forty nights until he reached Horeb, the mountain of God. There he went into a cave and spent the night" (19:9). In the strength of God's angel food, Elijah journeyed into the wilderness to Mount Horeb (Sinai), the mountain of revelation, where God always spoke his mind. There the Lord addressed the deeper elements of Elijah's discouragement.

> And the word of the Lord came to him: "What are you doing here, Elijah?" He replied, "I have been very zealous for the LORD God Almighty. The Israelites have rejected your covenant, broken down your altars, and put your prophets to death with the sword. I am the only one left, and now they are trying to kill me too." The LORD said, "Go out and stand on the mountain in the presence of the LORD, for the LORD is about to pass by." Then a great and powerful wind tore the mountains apart and shattered the rocks before the LORD, but the LORD was not in the wind. After the wind there was an earthquake, but the LORD was not in the earthquake. After the earthquake came a fire, but the LORD was not in the fire. And after the fire came a gentle whisper. When Elijah heard it, he

pulled his cloak over his face and went out and stood
at the mouth of the cave. Then a voice said to him,
"What are you doing here, Elijah?" (19:9–13).

"The Lord is going to pass by," Elijah was assured, and so
he looked for signs of God's passing. First there were winds
of hurricane force, then a devastating earthquake and a fire
storm of titanic proportion. But in each God was conspicuous
by his absence. When he did pass by, Elijah saw nothing, felt
nothing. The only evidence of God was a still, small voice—a
nearly inaudible whisper.

You never know about God: He may appear in
extraordinary and melodramatic ways—in hurricane,
earthquake, or storm. But he's usually much less obvious.
God's heroics, when they appear, are rarely as expected. He
works in quietness, his Spirit gently wafting like the wind,
here and there, touching one, touching another, working in
silence to get his work done. The obvious is usually spurious.
God's best efforts are rarely seen. That's the word from
Sinai.

The problem with Elijah was that he had wholly
unrealistic expectations of God. He had seen the Lord
manifest himself in stupendous display on Mount Carmel. He
expected a repeat performance—that God would make short
work of Jezebel, blasting her off the face of the earth with a
fireball. But instead of a lightning bolt, Jezebel got God's
forbearance and Elijah got a contract on his life. He collapsed
into disappointment and depression.

God's way of correcting Elijah's perspective was to bring
him to the place of revelation, which is what he must do with
us again and again. It's in that quiet place that we hear God's
voice. That's where we hear the truth, the whole truth and
nothing but the truth. That's where we get real.

Folk Christianity—that perspective nowhere taught in the
Bible, but generally believed—says that everyone is a winner:

no one gets Alzheimer's disease, no one dies from cancer, no one fails in marriage, no one falls to mental illness. Everyone lives happily ever after. But that's not the way it is.

Life is difficult. "The world is painful in any case; but it is quite unbearable if anybody gives us the idea that we are meant to be liking it," Charles Williams said. When people tell me that life is hard, I reply, "Of course it is." I find that answer more satisfying than anything else I can say. Every year confirms my belief that life is difficult and demanding. Any other response is unrealistic.

Life rarely goes as we think it should. We lose our jobs; we lose our health; we lose our children, one way or another. Our stocks fall, our retirement plans fail, our dreams go belly up.

We labor long hours with only fragmentary results. We're disregarded and ignored, slandered and maligned; we get trampled on by insensitive people. Some days we fall flat on our faces. Our best efforts are a disaster, our best foot forward becomes a bitter embarrassment. As my friend Fred Smith says, "Anything is possible with God, even failure."

But not to worry: The events that we call tragedies, setbacks, and failures are opportunities for God. He knows how to draw glory even from our ruin. "Not to be downcast after failure is one of the marks of true sanctity" (Dom Augustine Guillerand).

The hour of deepest humiliation, when we feel defective and utterly disqualified may be the hour that God uses us in unparalleled ways. Years of "wasted" effort may be the years when God plants an eternal harvest.

There's more going on than we can ever know. Though we think our efforts have been in vain, there's something in the wind. God's Spirit is wafting about, deftly and tenderly touching others, touching us, making us more like him than we ever thought possible, using us to influence others in ways we never imagined.

He is at work, if not in the strong winds then in the gentle zephyr; if not in the earthquake then in our heartbreak; in crowds or lonely hearts.

The "wind blows where it will." We can't control it; we can only believe that it is true. That's the perspective Elijah learned in that quiet place; that's what we learn.

> *So let the noise subside,*
> *And listen deep inside;*
> *He will speak; he will speak.*
>
> *But it won't be an earthquake;*
> *And it won't be fire;*
> *Or the whirling wind;*
> *Taking you higher.*
> *It will be a still small voice;*
> *And you'll have no choice;*
> *But to hear; but to hear.*

—John Fischer

One way to get going

Elijah missed the message. When asked again, "What are you doing here, Elijah?" he repeated himself, "I have been very zealous for the LORD God Almighty. The Israelites have rejected your covenant, broken down your altars, and put your prophets to death with the sword. I am the only one left, and now they are trying to kill me too."

"The Lord said to him, 'Go back the way you came, and go to the Desert of Damascus. When you get there, anoint Hazael king over Aram. Also, anoint Jehu son of Nimshi king over Israel, and anoint Elisha son of Shephat from Abel Meholah to succeed you as prophet. Jehu will put to death any who escape the sword of Hazael, and Elisha will put to death any who escape the sword of Jehu. Yet I reserve seven thousand in Israel—all whose knees have not bowed down to Baal and all whose mouths have not kissed him" (19:15–18).

God's word was insistent: "Go back! You still have work to do!" There were things of great importance for Elijah to do: He was to anoint Hazael, the Syrian king who unwittingly became Elijah's ally in the struggle against Israel and Ahab (2 Kings 13:22). He was to anoint Jehu king over Israel, the man who eventually brought the evil Jezebel to her well-deserved end. He was to anoint Elisha, his companion in ministry and successor to it.

Furthermore, God assured Elijah that he was not alone; he was part of a significant whole. There were yet thousands in Israel—"all whose knees have not bowed down to Baal and all whose mouths have not kissed him."

Elijah couldn't master his emotions and snap out of his dark mood; not even God would insist upon it. Nor did God's word immediately take hold. Our emotions are beyond our control and black moods can continue long after the causes of depression are removed. Sadness needs its time to be.

No, Elijah wasn't asked to alter his mood, but he was asked to choose—his will was operative. A century ago, British minister Francis Paget said, "It may be impossible at times to feel what one would; it is not impossible to will what one should; and that, if the will be real and honest, is what matters most."

John White writes, "There is no place for giving up. The warfare is much bigger than our personal humiliations. To feel sorry for oneself is totally inappropriate. Over such a soldier I would pour a bucket of icy water. I would drag him to his feet, kick him in the rear end and put his sword in his hand and shout, 'Now fight!' In some circumstances one must be cruel to be kind. What if you've fallen for a tempting ruse of the Enemy? What if you're not the most brilliant swordsman in the army? You hold Excaliber in your hand. Get behind the lines for a break if you're too weak to go on and strengthen yourself with a powerful draught of Romans 8:1–4. Then get back into the fight before your muscles get stiff!"

We can get back into the fight if we will. And therein lies the rub: Do we want to deal with our discouragement? Blue moods can initially be pleasurable; pandering to our misery and nursing self-pity feels good for a season. But like all illicit pleasure, the aftertaste is bitter. Sowing to one's own flesh inevitably leads to corruption (Galatians 6:8–10).

We must decide that despair must go. We must not be passive and wait for it to go away by itself. We must learn to battle fiercely against discouragement. We must stay near the place of revelation, sit at our Lord's feet and listen to his words. He reminds us there of the things that matter: who he is, what he has done and what he is doing. It's there that we get his perspective, regain our focus, and re-establish our priorities. In that quiet place we hear again, "The one who calls you is faithful and *he* will do it" (1 Thessalonians 5:24).

We must get up and get going. There's always something God is asking us to do, something as simple as going to work. He only asks us to do what he empowers us to do. We must shake off our lethargy and, like that other cripple whom Jesus restored, get up from our beds and *walk*. It's necessary for us to take that first step, for God "will carry us in his arms till we are able to walk and he will carry us in his arms when we are weary and cannot walk; but he will not carry us if we will not walk" (George MacDonald).

Hard to do? Indeed it is! Like plunging into an icy stream. But it can be done. When we choose to do his will, God gives us what we need to comply. Our feelings may lag. Our dark mood may linger. But God will indeed carry us in his arms until we're back on our feet. And so, "Elijah *went* from there. . . ." (19:19). He got back into the action. Will you?

Moses

ANY OLD BUSH WILL DO

For what are they all in their high conceit,
When man in the bush with God may meet?

—Ralph Waldo Emerson

When I was a student at the University of California in Berkeley I took a course in Ugaritic, one of the languages of the ancient Canaanites.

One day we translated a small tablet from a Canaanite temple. It was a prayer, written and left at the feet of an idol. It read as follows: "O El, cut through my stammering; remove the impediment." Here was a pitiable Canaanite, humiliated by his affliction, imploring the god El to heal him. That's what you would expect a pagan god to do.

But our God has other ideas. He does not necessarily cure us of our handicaps. He rather puts them to his intended use. Look at Moses' case.

One popular Jewish legend explains that Moses burned his tongue on a hot coal in infancy and was left with a speech impediment for the rest of his life. The legend reflects an ancient and widely held belief, based on Moses' prayer in Exodus 4:10: "O Lord, I have never been eloquent, neither in the past nor since you have spoken to your servant. I am slow of speech and tongue" and his complaint on two other occasions: "I speak with faltering lips" (Exodus 6:12, 30).

Recent studies suggest that the ancient authorities were right in believing that Moses had a speech defect. They put the expression "slow of speech and tongue" squarely in the realm of ancient medical terminology describing a speech impediment. We have no way of knowing what Moses' defect was, but it must have been severe: perhaps he stammered.

How humiliating to appear before the Pharaoh of Egypt in his great palace at Karnak, surrounded by the pomp of that place and stutter out his demand: "L-l-let my p-p-p-people g-g-go!"

Yet this was the man God used to do something for which there is no analogy in history before his time or after.

Mission impossible

Now Moses was tending the flock of Jethro his father-in-law, the priest of Midian, and he led the flock to the far side of the desert and came to Horeb, the mountain of God (Exodus 3:1).

The story begins in the back side of the deep desert where Moses was working for his father-in-law, Jethro. For forty years, Moses had herded Jethro's flock—forty long years of relentless, dreary duty.

Once Moses had been part of Egypt's aristocracy, educated and finished in the best Egyptian schools ready for anything. Now he was nothing but a ragged sheepherder. Now he had no confidence in himself. Now God could get to work.

God began on a day like any other day. The sun rose in a cloudless sky, throwing its searing heat on the broken wasteland below. Moses' sheep grazed as usual on the sparse vegetation or lay panting under some scant patch of shade. The looming mountains, the withering sun, the terrible silence—everything continued as it had since the beginning of time.

Then suddenly, an ordinary desert bush burst into flame. Moses saw the bush ablaze and went off to investigate. Clearly this was no ordinary plant, for though it burned it was not consumed!

> "I will go over and see this strange sight—why the bush does not burn up."
>
> When the LORD saw that he had gone over to look, God called to him from within the bush, "Moses! Moses!"
>
> And Moses said, "Here I am."
>
> "Do not come any closer." God said. "Take off your sandals, for the place where you are standing is holy ground." Then he said, "I am the God of your father, the God of Abraham, the God of Isaac and the God of Jacob." At this, Moses hid his face, because he was afraid to look at God.
>
> The LORD said, "I have indeed seen the misery of my people in Egypt. I have heard them crying out because of their slave drivers, and I am concerned about their suffering. So I have come down to rescue them from the hand of the Egyptians and to bring them up out of that land into a good and spacious land, a land flowing with milk and honey—the home of the Canaanites, Hittites, Amorites, Perizzites, Hivites and Jebusites. And now the cry of the Israelites has reached me, and I have seen the way the Egyptians are oppressing them. So now, go. I am sending you to Pharaoh to bring my people the Israelites out of Egypt" (3:3–10).

The great pharaohs of the eighteenth or nineteenth dynasty were ruling in Egypt at this time. They were the most powerful and prestigious rulers in the ancient world. Their empire stretched from Egypt to the Euphrates and into the Mediterranean, including the islands of Cyprus and Crete. They had enslaved and ruled Israel for four hundred years. How could Moses save them? His hands and tongue were tied.

That's the way it is with God: he chooses the most inapt and inept men to do the most impossible things. "So now, go," he says, "I am sending *you* to Pharaoh to bring my people the Israelites out of Egypt."

Who am I?

Moses had a problem with that mandate:

> But Moses said to God, "Who am I, that I should go to Pharaoh and bring the Israelites out of Egypt?"
> And God said, "I will be with you. And this will be the sign to you that it is I who have sent you: When you have brought the people out of Egypt, you will worship God on this mountain" (3:11–12).

Had God called Moses forty years earlier he would have been much too eager to comply. With his background, training, and connections in the court he was the perfect solution. He was God's man for the job! But now Moses was full of disclaimer and doubt. Disappointment and failure, the loneliness of the desert and the silence of God had shattered his sense of worth: "Who am I," he asked, "that I should go to Pharaoh and bring the Israelites out of Egypt" (3:11).

God's way of establishing Moses' self-worth was not to enumerate the man's assets and abilities, which is what we normally do to prop up someone's sagging ego. Rather, God assured Moses that he was present. "I will be with you!" he promised (3:12). It didn't matter at all who Moses was. What mattered was that God was with him.

He is with you today. God says insistently and firmly, "Surely I am with you always, to the very end of the age" (Matthew 28:20). That's not a figure of speech; it's a fact. He is present in a literal, spatial, local sense, more real than any other reality.

When Jesus met with his disciples in the Upper Room he left them with this consolation: "I will ask the Father, and he will give you another Counselor to be with you forever—the Spirit of truth. The world cannot accept him, because it neither sees him nor knows him. But you know him, for he lives with you and will be in you. I will not leave you as orphans; *I will come to you*" (John 14:16–18). This is not our Lord's Second Coming but his coming at Pentecost to be with his own.

Jesus came and went several times before he ascended to get that lesson into his disciples' minds: even though they could not see him, he was as close to them as he had been in the days of his flesh.

According to the gospel narratives, when Jesus ascended he rose vertically for a short distance and then *disappeared* into thin air. He did not pass into outer space like an ascending rocket. Rather, he stepped out of the realm of the seen into that unseen dimension around us which the Scriptures invite us to "see" through the eyes of faith (2 Corinthians 4:18; Hebrews 11:27).

This means that Jesus is as close to us as he was in the days of his flesh though invisible to our natural eyes. "Where'er we tread 'tis holy ground," Byron said. Every inch of space is crammed with his presence.

He is with us every moment of our lives. There is not one hour without his presence, not one mile without his companionship. He will never leave us nor will he ever forsake us. "So we say with confidence, 'The Lord is my helper; I will not be afraid' " (Hebrews 13:6).

Who are you?

> Moses [then] said to God, "Suppose I go to the Israelites and say to them, 'The God of your fathers has sent me to you,' and they ask me, 'What is his name?' Then what shall I tell them?"
>
> God said to Moses, "I AM WHO I AM. This is what you are to say to the Israelites: 'I AM has sent me to you.' "
>
> God also said to Moses, "Say to the Israelites, 'The LORD, the God of your fathers—the God of Abraham, the God of Isaac and the God of Jacob—has sent me to you.' This is my name forever, the name by which I am to be remembered from generation to generation (Exodus 3:13–15).

Moses said, "Suppose I go to the Israelites and say to them, 'The God of your fathers has sent me to you,' and they will say to me, 'What is his name?' Then what shall I tell them?" Note the progression: "If it makes no difference who *I* am—then *who are you?*" "What is your name?"

Yahweh's name was not unknown to Moses. His mother's name, Jachebed means "Yahweh is my glory." No, Moses knew the name. His question was, "What is the *meaning* of your name? (The particular Hebrew interrogative he uses makes that clear.) God patiently explained: his name means, "I AM."

God's name, usually translated *Yahweh*, is related to the Hebrew verb, "to be." (It's the verb used in verse 12: "I will be with you.") Thus God declares, "*I AM* [is] WHO I AM." "This is what you are to say to the Israelites: I AM has sent me to you' " (3:14).

What does he mean by naming himself, "I AM?" Simply this: "I am whatever you need."

Are you weary? He is rest. Are you unloved? He is love. Are you inadequate? He is sufficient. Are you perplexed? He

Are you inadequate? He is sufficient. Are you perplexed? He is wisdom. Are you pressured and out of sorts? He is peace. Are you guilty? He is your place of forgiveness (1 John 1:9).

> *Wisdom, righteousness and power*
> *Holiness for every hour*
> *My redemption full and free*
> *He is all I need.*

—Author unknown

I AM is God's name forever—the name by which he was to be remembered from generation to generation. Moses' whole life was inspired by that name. Slowly it made its way into the fabric of his mind. In time he learned that God was all he needed. That was the thought that sustained him.

And so it is for you this day. Do you feel set aside, displaced, without a place to serve? Do you believe your limitations and impediments have made you helpless? Think again. He is all you need.

What is in your hand?

> Moses answered, "What if they do not believe me or listen to me and say, 'The LORD did not appear to you'?"
>
> Then the LORD said to him, "What is that in your hand?"
>
> "A staff," he replied.
>
> The LORD said, "Throw it on the ground."
>
> Moses threw it on the ground and it became a snake, and he ran from it. Then the LORD said to him, "Reach out your hand and take it by the tail." So Moses reached out and took hold of the snake and it turned back into a staff in his hand. "This," said the

LORD, "is so that they may believe that the LORD, the
God of their fathers—the God of Abraham, the God
of Isaac and the God of Jacob—has appeared to you."

Then the LORD said, "Put your hand inside your
cloak." So Moses put his hand into his cloak, and
when he took it out, it was leprous, like snow.

"Now put it back into your cloak," he said. So
Moses put his hand back into his cloak, and when he
took it out, it was restored, like the rest of his flesh.

Then the LORD said, "If they do not believe you or
pay attention to the first miraculous sign, they may
believe the second. But if they do not believe these
two signs or listen to you, take some water from the
Nile and pour it on the dry ground. The water you
take from the river will become blood on the ground"
(Exodus 4:1–9).

Moses was still wary: "What if they [the elders of Israel]
do not believe me or listen to me and say, 'The Lord did not
appear to you'?" (He had not appeared for 400 years.) Moses'
question had to do with his authority: He had no power base,
no political clout. He was a backward, bashful man. Who
would listen to the likes of him?

God's answer came in the form of three signs, all of
which attested to Moses' ability to do what no human being
could do (4:2–8). These were the guarantees that God was
with him.

God asked, "What is that in your hand?" And Moses
replied, "A staff." It was only his shepherd's crook, but what
a history could be written of it: cast to the ground to become a
serpent, then taken up again as a mere staff; stretched out over
the Red Sea to point out a pathway through its depths; struck
against the flinty rock from which water gushed for the thirsty
crowd; raised in intercession over Israel as they defeated
Amalek in bloody conflict. It was only a stick, but in Moses'

hand it became a mighty symbol of the power and presence of God.

"Put your hand inside your cloak," God said. "So Moses put his hand into his cloak, and when he took it out, it was leprous, like snow." Then he was told to put his hand again inside his cloak and his leprosy was healed. Never in history had anyone been healed of leprosy.

The third sign, the power to turn the Nile River into blood, was a vivid touch, a terrible omen to the people of that land who depended entirely on the river and worshiped it as a god.

We do well to ponder these symbols. They tell us that our influence on others is based not on wholeness of body and mind. Nor is it dependent on our training, background, experience, intelligence, or appearance, but on miracles wrought by God.

The greatest miracle is the work that God is doing in our souls to conform our character to his. He creates the good works in which we walk; he changes us and that change is efficacious: it attracts the attention of others and makes them attentive to what we have to say. There is nothing quite so powerful as a truly godly man.

In 1966, during the closing service of the World Congress on Evangelism in the Kongresshalle in Berlin, Germany, Billy Graham spoke of the need for "a gentleness and a kindness and a love and a forgiveness and a compassion" that will mark us as different from the world. He concluded, "We must be a holy people."

As an illustration of the power of personal holiness, he spoke of the conversion of Dr. H. C. Morrison, founder of Asbury Theological Seminary. He described a day many years ago when Morrison as a farm worker was plowing in a field. Looking down the road, he saw an old Methodist circuit rider coming by on his horse. Morrison had seen the elderly gentleman before and he knew him to be a gracious, godly person. As he watched the old saint go by, Morrison felt the power of God's presence, and a great sense of conviction of sin came over him and he dropped to his knees. There between the furrows in his field, alone, he gave his life to God. When Dr. Graham concluded the story he earnestly prayed, "Oh, God, make me a holy man—a holy man."

May God create in us that holiness that will persuade others toward God and his righteousness.

Tongue tied

Moses' fear lingered on: "O Lord, I have never been eloquent, neither in the past nor since you have spoken to your servant. I am slow of speech and tongue" (4:10).

Ah, here we have it: the reason Moses demurred. He was ashamed of his affliction, unwilling to expose himself to humiliation by speaking in Pharaoh's court.

But hear what God says to Moses: "The LORD said to him 'Who gave man his mouth? Who makes him deaf or dumb? Who gives him sight or makes him blind? Is it not I, the LORD? Now go; I will help you speak and I will teach you what to say" (4:11–12).

God was not at all concerned about Moses' impediment. He had, in fact, given it to him! His speech defect was a divinely created deficiency. Moses' impediment might frustrate him, but it could not frustrate God.

Our impairments, disabilities, and handicaps are not accidents. They are God-designed. He creates every one of our flaws out of infinite wisdom. God's way of dealing with our afflictions is not to remove them but to endow them with strength and utilize them for good.

Paul said of his handicap: "Three times I pleaded with the Lord to take it away from me. But he said to me, 'My grace is sufficient for you, for my power is made perfect in weakness.' Therefore," Paul concluded, "I will boast all the more gladly about my weaknesses, so that Christ's power may rest on me. That is why, for Christ's sake, I delight in weaknesses . . . . For when I am weak, then I am strong" (2 Corinthians 12:8–10).

Matthew Henry wrote, "A great deal of wisdom and true worth may be with a slow tongue. God sometimes makes choice of those as his messengers, who have the least of the advantages of art or nature, that his grace in them may appear the more glorious."

Ruth Bell Graham makes the same point in one of her poems:

> *He is not eloquent*
> *as men count such;*
> *for him*
> *words trip and stumble*
> *giving speech*
> *an awkward touch,*
> *and humble:*
> *so, much*
> *is left unsaid*
> *that he would say*
> *if he were eloquent.*
> *Wisely discontent,*
> *compassion driven*
> *(as avarice drives some,*
> *ambition others),*
> *the old, the lonely,*
> *and the outcast come;*
> *all are welcome,*
> *all find a home,*
> *all—his brothers.*
>
> *Behind him*
> *deeds rise quietly*
> *to stay;*

and those with eyes to see
can see
all he can say.

Perhaps he'd not have spent
his life this way
if he were eloquent.

—Ruth Bell Graham

Moses' inadequacy was God's opportunity. God's strength was made perfect through Moses' weakness. Words would be given to him—as they will be given to you. You will be enriched in every way: "in all your speaking and in all knowledge" (1 Corinthians 1:5).

He who made your body can manifest his beauty in it. He who made your mouth can put his words into it. Ask him to make himself visible in you. Ask him to speak to you that you may speak to others. "It will not be you speaking, but the Spirit of your Father speaking through you" (Matthew 10:20).

What we say matters far more to God than how we say it. Certainly, we can all learn to speak with greater clarity and simplicity; however, God is not looking for oratory and eloquence but substance and Spirit.

We must get our message straight from God. What he has to say to us directly is what we have to say to others. Commentaries, books, notes from other teachers are valuable, but the most powerful truths are those that God has been teaching to you. Wait before him in silence until he gives you something to say. In that quiet place of revelation—reading and meditating on his words—he will enrich you in all your speaking and in all your knowledge.

George MacDonald said, "There is a chamber—a chamber in God himself which none can enter but the one, the individual, the particular man. Out of which chamber that man has to bring revelation and strength for his brethren. This is that for which he was made—to reveal the secret things of the Father." This is the place of deep wisdom and profound simplicity from which we go to give utterance to what we have seen and heard.

When you have heard what God has to say, rely on his Spirit in its proclamation. There is a force at work, more subtle, more powerful and penetrating, far greater than human perfection. When God's Spirit certifies our words, strange things begin to happen to those who hear them; strong influences begin to play upon their hearts—influences that touch the conscience at its deepest levels.

What ties God's hands?

There's a final note. Moses, still unpersuaded, carries on: " 'O Lord, please send someone else to do it.' Then, the LORD's anger burned against Moses" (4:13–14).

How odd of God to be outraged now, to tolerate Moses' deficiencies and doubts, but to fume when he passes the buck. But Moses is now guilty of serious sin. The only thing that frustrates God and ties his hands is when we declare ourselves unavailable.

George McDonald put it well: "God will carry us in his arms if we cannot walk; he will carry us in his arms until we can walk; but he will not carry us if we will not walk."

HEIGH HO! HEIGH HO! IT'S OFF TO WORK WE GO

Rest and be thankful.

—Inscription on a stone seat in the Highlands of Scotland

There was this fellow Moses knew who went out to pick up sticks on the Sabbath to build a fire and warm his hands:

Those who found him gathering wood brought him to Moses and Aaron and the whole assembly and they kept him in custody, because it was not clear what should be done to him. Then the LORD said to Moses, 'The man must die' (Numbers 15:32–36).

"Good grief," Charlie Brown would say. This man's offense seems so trifling and yet he's guilty of a capitol crime! "More must be meant than meets the ear," Milton said.

Indeed there is, though it may be enough at this point to say that working too hard is a dangerous occupation—hazardous to your health, you might say.

I must admit, however, that I'm a workaholic at heart. But I'm in good company. As James Taylor would say, "There's a holy host of others standin' round me." Most of us are driven, compulsive performers, and unfortunately our work habits carry over into our walk with God and our work for him. We're driven and compulsive in our faith and service— always hustling and hoping to do more.

Jesus was never that busy. You just don't see him rushing around like we do. He had an infinite job to do and only three and a half years to do it, and yet there was hardly a trace of effort in his work. Even when people made impossible demands of him, his pace was measured and slow. In fact, the only person he ever told to get busy was Judas: "What you are about to do, do quickly," he said (John 13:27).

Someone has said that "busy Christian" ought to sound to us like "adulterous wife." The two ideas are utterly incongruent. Busyness is not a Christian virtue, and spiritual maturity is not measured by the amount of work we do, no matter what we're busy doing or how much we get done. There's more to the Christian life than increasing its speed.

Thomas Merton has written with great wisdom,

> *To allow one's self to be carried away*
> 　　*by a multitude of conflicting concerns,*
> *To surrender to too many demands,*
> *To commit one's self to too many projects,*
> *To want to help everyone in everything,*
> 　　*is to succumb to violence.*
> *Frenzy destroys our inner capacity for peace.*
> *It destroys the fruitfulness of our work*
> 　　*because it kills the root of inner wisdom*
> 　　*which makes work fruitful.*

Most of us, however, though we know better, can't let up. Life for us is one prolonged and dedicated struggle to fix everything that's broken and achieve perfection in all we do, no matter how much it takes out of us. We have to keep hustling and hoping to do more—more than God ever intended for us to do, more than God ever designed our bodies to do—a condition a friend of mine calls "hyper-living." That's why we get so weary and worn-out, and that's why we want to quit. What we need is rest.

Remember the Sabbath

There's a God-given method for relieving fatigue. Israel's prophets called it *Shabbat*. That's where we get our English word, *Sabbath*. Essentially it means "to cease and desist." "Cessation of work with accompanying rest" is the connotation.

Shabbat is the oldest and most important institution in the world. It was established in the beginning:

By the seventh day God had finished the work he had been doing; so on the seventh day he rested from all his work. And God blessed the seventh day and made it holy, because on it he rested from all the work of creating that he had done (Genesis 2:2–3).

Genesis 1 describes God's handiwork. For six days God worked to create a world of enjoyment for his children. Then on the seventh day he took a breather to relax and luxuriate in what he had done.

God gave his day of rest special prominence and significance: He blessed it and made it *different*, the common-place meaning of the word *holy*. The Sabbath was unique and novel, absolutely unlike any other day.

In the beginning God established a rhythm in the cosmos—six days of work and one day of rest. He did so by example and decree, writing that cadence large on our calendars.

The phrase "there was evening and there was morning" is conspicuously absent on the seventh day. The seventh day has a beginning, but it goes on forever—an eternal pause from work. There is simply no end to God's rest.

Ancient history

The notion of a restful seventh day is rooted deep in human memory and history. Very early Mesopotamian cuneiform tablets contain calendars in which the seventh, fourteenth, twenty-first and twenty-eighth days are distinguished from the rest by rubrics. In several of those tablets the word *shabatum* appears, a word similar to the Hebrew *shabbat*.

In one tablet the *shabatum* is called *um nuch libbi* ("a day to rest the heart"). On those days kings were not permitted to discuss affairs of state, physicians couldn't care for the sick, and other proscriptions applied.

There are major differences between the Babylonian *shabbatum* and God's *shabbat*, not the least of which is the fact that the Babylonian sabbath applied only to royalty and to certain professionals and not to ordinary citizens. The common folk were drudges who toiled seven days a week.

Despite the differences in the two sabbaths, however, the fact remains that the notion of *Shabbat* was ingrained in the human race—a vestigial memory of God's created rhythm: six days of labor followed by one day of rest.

Manna and the morning after

The second reference to the Sabbath occurs in a context of gathering and preparing manna. The word *Shabbat* occurs in the biblical text here for the first time, though the idea is clearly inferred from the creation story.

Each morning everyone gathered as much [manna] as he needed, and when the sun grew hot, it melted away. On the sixth day, they gathered twice as much—two omers for each person—and the leaders of the community came and reported this to Moses. He said to them, "This is what the LORD commanded: 'Tomorrow is to be a day of rest, a holy Sabbath to the LORD. So bake what you want to bake and boil what you want to boil. Save whatever is left and keep it until morning.' "

So they saved it until morning, as Moses commanded, and it did not stink or get maggots in it. "Eat it today," Moses said, "because today is a Sabbath to the LORD. You will not find any of it on the ground today. Six days you are to gather it, but on the seventh day, the Sabbath, there will not be any (Exodus 16:21–30).

For six days the sons of Israel gathered manna. Each day brought its own supply—as much as anyone could eat. The lesson of trust for daily bread was constantly being enforced: each day came and the manna fell.

On the sixth morning twice as much manna lay waiting on the sands of the desert. God had been at work through the night, anticipating his children's needs, providing up front so they could rest and enjoy his Sabbath.

The ten words

The fourth commandment codified the Sabbath and made it a distinctively Hebrew institution:

"Remember the Sabbath day by keeping it holy. Six days you shall labor and do all your work, but the seventh day is a Sabbath to the LORD your God. On it you shall not do any work, neither you, nor your son

or daughter, nor your manservant or maidservant, nor
your animals, nor the alien within your gates. For in
six days the LORD made the heavens and the earth, the
sea, and all that is in them, but he rested on the
seventh day. Therefore the LORD blessed the Sabbath
day and made it holy" (Exodus 20:8–11).

Here *Shabbat* is connected with God's seventh-day rest.
The Sabbath was a day to remember—to rest and relax
because God had done all that was necessary to do.

In Moses' later elaboration on this law, he insisted that
even in the busiest times of the year God wanted his children
to rest. "Six days you shall labor, but on the seventh day you
shall rest, *even during the plowing season and harvest* you
must rest," he insisted (Exodus 34:21).

Once more God wanted his children to know that even
when they were not working God was working to get their
work done.

Free at last!

The Sabbath law was reissued when Israel camped on the
plains of Moab:

"Observe the Sabbath day by keeping it holy, as the
LORD your God has commanded you. Six days you
shall labor and do all your work, but the seventh day
is a Sabbath to the LORD your God. On it you shall not
do any work, neither you, nor your son or daughter,
nor your manservant or maidservant, nor your ox,
your donkey or any of your animals, nor the alien
within your gates, so that your manservant and
maidservant may rest, as you do. Remember that you
were slaves in Egypt and that the LORD your God
brought you out of there with a mighty hand and an

outstretched arm. Therefore the LORD your God has commanded you to observe the Sabbath day" (Deuteronomy 5:12–15).

In the two biblical versions of the Sabbath law the commands are identical but the reasons differ. The reason in Exodus is that God created the world and everything in it for us to enjoy. The Deuteronomic reason for Sabbath-observance is that God has forever delivered his people from drudgery.

Israel's ancestors in Egypt went four hundred years without a vacation—they could never take a day off. They were chattel, doing mindless, menial tasks, making bricks without straw. Then God went to work and set them free. The Sabbath was a day to remember that great emancipation and the redemptive work he had done.

The sabbatical year

The principle of a recurring day of rest is extended to the land:

> "For six years sow your fields, and for six years prune your vineyards and gather their crops. But in the seventh year the land is to have a sabbath of rest, a sabbath to the LORD. Do not sow your fields or prune your vineyards" (Leviticus 25:3–4).

Every seventh year the land itself was to have a sabbath of rest from sowing and reaping, not so much for the sake of the land as for the laborers who worked it. Here's relief from the tyranny of production. God would see to it that the volunteer yield of the land would suffice:

> "You may ask, 'What will we eat in the seventh year if we do not plant or harvest our crops?' I will send

you such a blessing in the sixth year that the land will
yield enough for three years. While you plant during
the eighth year, you will eat from the old crop and
will continue to eat from it until the harvest of the
ninth year comes in' " (Leviticus 25:19–22).

This is the law of the manna on a larger scale (Exodus
16:22), the point of which once more is that while Israel
rested God was providing. Farmers could let the land lie
fallow and let God work their fields.

Canaan rest

God also taught *Shabbat* through the conquest and
settlement of Canaan:

"Remember the command that Moses the servant of
the LORD gave you: 'The LORD your God is giving you
rest and has granted you this land' " (Joshua 1:13).

When Israel was about to occupy the land they were told
that God would fight their battles for them, drive out the
Canaanites, guarantee their right to the land and give them
rest. In the end the Lord did just that: He "gave them rest on
every side, just as he had sworn to their forefathers. Not one
of their enemies withstood them; the LORD handed all their
enemies over to them" (Joshua 21:44).

Once again God preceded them, anticipating their needs:
"I sent the hornet ahead of you, which drove them out before
you," he said. "You did not do it with your own sword and
bow" (Joshua 24:12). God conquered Canaan; all Israel had
to do was enter in and enjoy the rest he had provided. For
twenty five years Israel had been fighting a battle that God
had already won.

The sign

The most significant of all Sabbath verses is sometimes overlooked:

> The Israelites are to observe the Sabbath, celebrating it for the generations to come as a lasting covenant. It will be a sign between me and the Israelites forever, for in six days the LORD made the heavens and the earth, and on the seventh day he abstained from work and rested (Exodus 31:16–17).

Here *Shabbat* is designated a "sign" of the covenant between God and Israel. Ezekiel expressed that idea more fully: "I gave them my Sabbaths as a sign between us, so they would know that I the LORD made them holy" (Ezekiel 20:12).

The sum of Ezekiel's argument is that the Sabbath was a sign or symbol to Israel of a greater reality: God is the one who sanctifies and sets men and women right. That's why Sabbath-keeping was so important; it connoted far more than it denoted. It signified the condition of one's heart. Those who kept *Shabbat* exemplified what it signified. They were resting in what God had done.

John Calvin said, "The Lord enjoined obedience to almost no other command as severely as to this [see Exodus 31:13; 35:2]. When he wills through the prophets to indicate that all religion has been overturned, he complains that his Sabbaths have been polluted, violated, not kept, not hallowed—as if, with this homage omitted, nothing more remained in which he could be honored [Isaiah 56:2; Jeremiah 17:21–22, 27; Ezekiel 20:12–13; 22:8; 23:38]."

And that's why Sabbath-breaking was serious sin: those who rejected *Shabbat* signified that they had not entered into God's rest. They were still trying to achieve salvation on their own.

The would-be woodcutter revisited

That's why so much severity was shown to the man who gathered wood on the Sabbath (Numbers 15). This man's lawlessness was not casual or accidental. It was intentional. The Hebrew verb translated "gathering" suggests *repetitive* wood-gathering, indicating this was more than a one-time excursion. It was a recurrent act. This man was flaunting his wood-gathering, demonstrating his intention to defy the law against lighting a fire on the Sabbath (Exodus 35:3). He was a determined, defiant "worker."

The story is actually an illustration of the difference between "unintentional" and "defiant" sin, spelled out in the preceding paragraph: "If just one person sins unintentionally, he must bring a year-old female goat for a sin offering. The priest is to make atonement before the LORD for the one who erred by sinning unintentionally, and when atonement has been made for him, he will be forgiven. . . . But anyone who sins defiantly, whether native-born or alien, blasphemes the LORD, and that person must be cut off from his people" (Numbers 15:27–30).

Unintentional is the wrong word, preserving, as it does, an old but false distinction between "witting" and "unwitting" sins. The Hebrew verb translated "unintentional" here means "to go astray" and can refer to serious, deliberate sins of the flesh—lying, theft, perjury, debauchery and the like—some of which are quite intentional and all of which can be forgiven (see Leviticus 6:1–7).

"Defiant" sin, on the other hand, is not a particular sin, but rather a disposition toward God. It is sinning "with a high hand"—raising one's fist and planting it in God's face. There was no forgiveness for this sin because the sinner had rejected the God who forgives. This is the sin (and the only sin) that Jesus describes as "unpardonable" (Matthew 12:31).

So, the Sabbath-breaker in this story was no ordinary sinner: He was a rebel, one of those who had refused to enter the land. There was something especially perverse about his resistance to God. He *would* not rest in God's provision and salvation. He was on his own, and that was (and still continues to be) serious sin.

Fringe benefits

Immediately afterward, the Lord commanded Moses to

"speak to the Israelites and say to them: 'Throughout the generations to come you are to make tassels on the corners of your garments, with a blue cord on each tassel. You will have these tassels to look at and so you will remember all the commands of the LORD, that you may obey them and not prostitute yourselves by going after the lusts of your own hearts and eyes. Then you will remember to obey all my commands and will be consecrated to your God. I am the LORD your God, who brought you out of Egypt to be your God. I am the LORD your God' " (Numbers 15:37–41).

These fringes were like the strings we tie on our fingers to remind us of things we must not forget. It's God's way of saying, "Never forget to remember the Sabbath!"

The point of the Sabbath

Before there was a single human being in the world to appreciate it God set apart the seventh day by example and precept. It was for the use and benefit of human race—a day of physical rest—but it was "meant to represent to the people of Israel *spiritual rest*, in which believers ought to lay aside their own works to allow God to work in them" (John Calvin, *Institutes* viii: 28).

Israel's symbolic Sabbath was God's way of getting his children to rest in what *he* was doing. He's knows our tendency to work ourselves to death. It's his way of saying, "Remember my work, relax and take delight in me" (Isaiah 58:13–14).

Jesus and the apostles

When you come to the New Testament you find Jesus and the apostles taking a rather cavalier attitude toward the Sabbath day. Our Lord himself periodically violated this most cherished of Israel's conventions, insisting that he had the right to do so because "the Son of Man is Lord of the Sabbath" (Matthew 12:8).

Paul abrogated Sabbath day observance declaring that observance of days is characteristic of those who are weak in the faith (Romans 14:1–5), who do not know that God has "canceled the written code, with its regulations, ... nailing it to the cross" (Colossians 2:14).

"Therefore," he goes on to say, "do not let anyone judge you by what you eat or drink, or with regard to a religious festival, a New Moon celebration or a Sabbath day. These are a shadow of the things that were to come; the reality, however, is found in Christ" (Colossians 2:16–17). The Sabbath day had been set aside since it was merely a shadow of something more substantial. Reality had come; the sign was no longer needed.

The first Christians took Paul's instruction to heart. They ignored the Sabbath day as a day, changing their time of worship to Sunday, the first day of the week. The Christian Sunday is not a continuation of the Jewish Sabbath "changed into the first day of the week," as one confession puts it, but rather a distinctively Christian institution adopted because Sunday was the day on which our Lord rose. That's why Sunday got the name, the "Lord's Day" (see Acts 20:7).

The creation of rest

The writer of Hebrews brings everything into focus. Thinking of those Israelites who perished in the wilderness he wrote,

> Who were they who heard and rebelled? Were they not all those Moses led out of Egypt? And with whom was he angry for forty years? Was it not with those who sinned, whose bodies fell in the desert? And to whom did God swear that they would never enter his rest if not to those who disobeyed? So we see that they were not able to enter, because of their unbelief.
>
> Therefore, since the promise of entering his rest still stands, let us be careful that none of you be found to have fallen short of it. For we also have had the gospel preached to us, just as they did; but the message they heard was of no value to them, because those who heard did not combine it with faith. Now we who have believed enter that rest, just as God has said,
>
> "So I declared on oath in my anger,
> 'They shall never enter my rest.' "
>
> And yet his work has been finished since the creation of the world. For somewhere he has spoken about the seventh day in these words: "And on the seventh day God rested from all his work" (Hebrews 3:16–4:4).

The author quotes from the creation story and insists that God's "work has been finished since the creation of the world."

Then he quotes from Psalm 95:7–8 and its implied promise of rest for the believers in David's day: "*Today*, if you hear his voice, do not harden your hearts as you did at Meribah, as you did that day at Massah in the desert."

God's offer of rest was not exhausted by Joshua's conquest of Canaan because the "rest" was still being extended to Israel in David's day, four hundred years after Joshua. Furthermore, he insists, that rest "still stands" (4:1). It is, in fact, a *sabbaton*—a word usually translated "Sabbath observance," but which implies *perpetual* Sabbath (4:9).

Here is the reality: God is for us and has been working for us from the beginning. Our salvation, our sanctification, our glorification is accomplished by believing in what he has done. Rest is all we have to do. "Anyone who enters God's rest also rests from his own work, just as God did from his" (Hebrews 4:10).

Doing the work of God

Some Jews once asked Jesus how they could "do God's work." He replied, "The work of God is this: to believe in the one he has sent" (John 6:29).

How audacious to think that any human being can do the works of God. Only God can do his works. Our work is not to do his work, but to believe that he has done everything that has to be done and can ever be done to bring salvation to us.

The Lord focused his anger on the Pharisees who burdened his people with effort-ridden activity, but he was never angry with those who were so burdened. He called them to come to him for rest.

"Come to me, all you who are weary and burdened, and I will give you rest. Take my yoke upon you and learn from me, for I am gentle and humble in heart, and you will find rest for your souls. For my yoke is easy and my burden is light" (Matthew 11:28–30).

Shabbat

Shabbat is not a day; it's a disposition, a mind-set of resting in God for everything we have to do, believing that God is at the heart of all our activity and that all the demands upon us are in fact demands upon him.

Shabbat is a profound conviction that God is working while we rest, a serene belief that there is a strong, experienced hand at the helm, a tacit understanding that God is working out everything for good.

Shabbat is rest from our labor. It is an unencumbered, unhurried, relaxed lifestyle that grows out of a profound awareness that "it is God who works in [us] to will and to act according to his good purpose" (Philippians 2:13). F. B. Meyer says,

> We must remember to maintain within our hearts the spirit of Sabbath calm and peace, not fussy, not anxious, nor fretful nor impetuous; refraining our feet from our own paths, our hand from our own devices, refusing to make our own joy and do our own works. It is only when we are fully resolved to act thus, allowing God to originate his own plans and to work in us for their accomplishment that we enter into our inheritance. . . . Be full of God's rest. Let there be no hurry, precipitation or fret; yield to God's hands that he may mold thee; hush thy quickly throbbing pulse. So shalt thou build to good and everlasting purpose.

Building to good and everlasting purpose

The prophet said to David, "You will have a son who will be a man of peace and rest. . . . He is the one who will build" (1 Chronicles 22:9–10). It is restful men who build enduring structures.

Solomon understood:

> Unless the LORD builds the house,
>   its builders labor in vain.
> Unless the LORD watches over the city,
>   the watchmen stand guard in vain.
> In vain you rise early and stay up late,
>   toiling for food to eat—
> for he grants sleep to those he loves
> (Psalm 127:1–3).

Who builds? The builder does, but unless God builds, the builder's labor is in vain. Who watches? The watchman does, but unless God watches the watchman stands guard in vain. Solomon's conclusion: It's senseless to stay up late, toiling for food. Go to sleep and let God work.

There's something wonderfully significant about this psalm—something easily missed unless we understand that *Shabbat* for Israel began, not on Saturday morning, but on Friday evening at bedtime.

The Hebrew evening and morning sequence says something significant to us: God puts his children to sleep so he can get his work done. "Sleep is God's contrivance for giving us the help he cannot get into us when we are awake," said George MacDonald.

In the evening fatigue overtakes us and we have to stop working. We lay ourselves down to sleep and drift off into blessed oblivion for the next six to eight hours, a state in which we are totally nonproductive. But nothing essential stops. Though we may leave many things undone and most projects unfinished, God is still on the job. "He gives to those he loves while they sleep." The next morning his eyes sweep over us and he awakens us to enjoy the benefits of all that he has done.

Most of us, however, hit the floor running. We wolf down a Pop-Tart™ and dash out the door clutching a travel mug of coffee. We have to be up and doing, getting things started and getting a world of things done.

That's because we do not understand that God has been working for us all along. We have awakened into a world in which everything was started centuries ago. God has been preparing the good works in which we find ourselves walking throughout the day.

> *Rest; rest in Him—*
> *Your work is through.*
> *Lean back on his great power;*
> *He'll work for you.*

—John Fischer

Examining our hearts

Why do we work so long and so hard? Why do we impose such tyrannical routines on ourselves? We know better; we talk about slowing down some day, but we never do. What are the motives that chain us to our desks twelve to eighteen hours of the day?

Charles Lamb asked, "Who first invented work and bound the free and holiday-rejoicing spirit down," and then blamed it all on "Sabbathless Satan" who tied us to "that dry drudgery at the desk's dark wood?" There's something to Lamb's conclusion; the devil is the one who plants in our heads the notion that everything depends on us.

But most of us can't complain too much about the devil. Our chains are self-imposed. Our work is our drug of choice, our escape from the perplexity and pain of the world. We're looking for a fix.

Or, we're looking for something *to* fix. We assume responsibility for everything. Our whole life is a struggle to make ourselves perfect and achieve perfection in others. We aim to set everything right that's wrong, forgetting that God is the only one who can set anything right. He's the fixer.

For some, work may be our sacrificial offering for sin, our expiation for the plagues of our past. Like monks in their cells we devote ourselves to drudgery, denying and flagellating ourselves, hoping somehow to save ourselves from past sin and guilt, or to prove that we're really not so bad after all.

For others, work provides opportunities to be important! We want to be wanted. That need creates the context in which we cultivate our work habits. We complain about call slips and incessant demand, but it's our need to be needed that drives the demand.

And then there are those of us who actually believe we're indispensable—that even God can't do without us. I recall praying with my wife, Carolyn, one night after returning from a weekend trip and thanking God for "taking care of things while I was gone," at which point Carolyn chuckled and wryly asked, "Who do you think takes care of things while you're here?" *Touché!*

Once we get it into our heads that God really doesn't need us to get his work done we can begin to deal with our manic work habits. We can take off now and then. We can take an hour each day or a portion of a day each week to be alone with God. We can take time to "howdy" with our friends and neighbors. We can take a vacation. We can miss a meeting or two. We can leave some tasks undone at the end of each day and go home. We can take time to talk and take long walks with our spouses and kids. We can hunt, fish, and golf with our friends.

Philipp Melanchthon once said to his friend Martin Luther, "Martin, this day we will discuss the governance of the universe." Luther replied, "This day you and I will go fishing and leave the governance of the universe to God."

We don't have to be dogged and driven by our work. The good news is God's *Shabbat.*

Finding rest

Our high-speed lives are essentially godless lives because we think we have no time to spend with God. But we all have time if we know that God is minding the store.

The fathers of the Church well understood the importance of what they called *otium sanctum* (holy leisure). They knew that we cannot give ourselves to spiritual things and deepen our relationship with him if we are obsessed with a multitude of things to do and always on the go. Love for God is a tender plant that can mature only when it has time to grow. God cannot be loved on the run.

I've come to see through the years that my own ministry is the greatest enemy of my love for God. I can get so busy doing things for him that I scarcely have time for him. My colleagues share my compulsions: we have calls to make, books to read, meetings to attend, messages to prepare. Our calendars are filled with appointments, our days are consumed with engagements, our minds are crammed with projects. There's scarcely a moment when we're not scheduled. We just don't have time for God.

But then I think of Jesus' friends, Mary and Martha, in whose home he was frequently entertained. He always found it perfectly suited to his needs. One day, while he was resting there, he began to teach Mary, who sat at his feet, knowing intuitively that there could be nothing more important to do than to listen to what he had to say.

But while Mary rested and listened to Jesus, Martha hustled about, "distracted by all the preparations that had to be made," trying to make the house more presentable, doing things for Jesus he didn't want done at all.

Finally Jesus told her in his kindly way that her busyness was much ado about nothing. "Martha, Martha," he said, "You are worried and upset about many things, but only one thing is needed. Mary has chosen what is better, and it will not be taken away from her" (Luke 10:41). We must not let the pressure of work take away from us "what is better."

Martha was busy and hurried,
Serving the friend divine,
Cleansing the cups and platters,
Bringing the bread and wine;
But Martha was careful and anxious
Fretted in thought and in word,
She had no time to be sitting
While she was serving the Lord,
For Martha was "cumbered" with "serving,"
Martha was "troubled" with "things"—
Those that would pass with the using—
She was forgetting her wings.

Mary was quiet and peaceful,
Learning to love and to live.
Mary was hearing His precepts,
Mary was letting Him give—
Give of the riches eternal,
Treasures of mind and of heart;
Learning the mind of the Master,
Choosing the better part.

Do we ever labor at serving
Till voices grow fretful and shrill,
Forgetting how to be loving,
Forgetting how to be still?
Do we strive for "things" in possession,
And toil for the perishing meat,
Neglecting the one thing needful—
Sitting at Jesus' feet?
Service is good when he asks it,
Labor is right in its place,

But there is one thing better,
Looking up in his face;
There is so much he can tell us,
Truths that are precious and deep;
This is the place where he wants us,
These are the things we can keep.

—Annie Johnson Flint

Holy leisure can be woven throughout the fabric of the day—a leisurely center in the midst of our work where just for a moment or two we draw near to the heart of God: remembering, reflecting, worshiping, centering on his presence.

Brother Lawrence describes this experience as "practicing the presence of God." He wrote, "I make it my business to persevere in his holy presence wherein I keep myself by a simple attention and a general fond regard to God, which I refer to as an actual presence of God. Or, to put it another way, an habitual, silent, and secret conversation of the soul with God."

David wrote: "I have set the LORD always before me. Because he is at my right hand, I will not be shaken. . . . You fill me with joy in your presence" (Psalm 16:8, 11).

Shabbat can lead us into an hour, an afternoon, a day, of solitude and silence: reading, praying, thinking, reflecting, journaling. A day to listen and receive, not for others but for the simple nurture of our own souls.

Shabbat can turn our Sunday into a Sabbath experience if we so choose—our day for worship, instruction, contemplation, and prayer. Paul, however, warns us not to turn our choice of a day into sabbatarianism and require it of ourselves or others. That's legalism—adding our requirements to God's Word—and puts us back into slavery. Any day will do.

Shabbat can result in time to cultivate relationships—with our family and other friends. Relationships don't just happen;

they are caused. And causation and cultivation take time, time we can afford if we know that God is staying on the job.

I have a self-employed friend who has decided to work four days each week so he can have three days a week to spend with his family. He may sacrifice some income, but, as he puts it, the benefits are better.

Shabbat can produce a day, an afternoon, or an hour simply to enjoy God's handiwork. What makes this a true Sabbath experience is relating everything to God's activity, thanking him in the course of the day and at the end of the day for all the joy he has brought into it—as David did:

> The heavens declare the glory of God;
>   the skies proclaim the work of his hands.
> Day after day they pour forth speech;
>   night after night they display knowledge
> (Psalm 19:1–2).

And then there are those Sabbath experiences that are pure fun: reading a Pat McManus book and laughing out loud, listening to Keith Green or Kenny G. or a bird sing in your back yard; walking a stream; playing a round of golf; running a river; tying a fly; taking a walk down the green belt with a friend (or without); puttering around in the yard; reading a child a book or reading a children's book; taking a nap.

Winnie-the-Pooh says, "Don't underestimate the value of Doing Nothing, of just going along, listening to all the things you can't hear, and not bothering." Let's hear it for Pooh! He understands *Shabbat*.

Caveats and cautions

We must not, however, understand *Shabbat* to mean lethargy or sloth, what Dorothy L. Sayers described as that "great, sprawling, lethargic sin." Sloth is one of the seven deadly sins.

The rhythm God created is *work* and rest. When we rest we ought to rest well; when we work, we ought to work hard. As old Satchel Paige used to say, "When I works, I works hard; when I sits, I sits loose."

A word for shirkers

In the name of the Lord Jesus Christ, we command you, brothers, to keep away from every brother who is idle and does not live according to the teaching you received from us. For you yourselves know how you ought to follow our example. We were not idle when we were with you, nor did we eat anyone's food without paying for it. On the contrary, we worked night and day, labouring and toiling so that we would not be a burden to any of you. We did this, not because we do not have the right to such help, but in order to make ourselves a model for you to follow. For even when we were with you, we gave you this rule: "If a man will not work [lit: "does not want to work"], he shall not eat."

We hear that some among you are idle. They are not busy; they are busybodies. Such people we command and urge in the Lord Jesus Christ to settle down and earn the bread they eat. And as for you, brothers, never tire of doing what is right.

If anyone does not obey our instruction in this letter, take special note of him. Do not associate with him, in order that he may feel ashamed. Yet do not regard him as an enemy, but warn him as a brother (2 Thessalonians 3:6–15).

This is not simply good advice; it is an apostolic command backed up by the authority of our Lord Jesus Christ. Charles Lamb notwithstanding, it wasn't "Sabbathless Satan" who "first invented work," but rather God, who saw its need. "Six days you shall labor," he said. We should, therefore, yield to Paul's exhortation to "settle down and *earn* the bread we eat."

Paul himself set the example:

> We were not idle when we were with you, nor did we eat anyone's food without paying for it. On the contrary, we worked night and day, laboring and toiling so that we would not be a burden to any of you. We did this, not because we did not have a right to such help, but in order make ourselves a model for you to follow (3:7–9).

Paul felt strongly about the need to work—so strongly that though he had the right to be supported in his ministry he set aside that right in order to set the pace for others. He paid the price to make his point.

A word for workers

"As for you, brothers, never tire of doing what is right [noble]" (3:13).

Work can be mindless and menial, offering little challenge or stimulation, and it can be humbling—pushing brooms or building widgets—but work done for God's sake is noble, no matter what you do.

Work is valuable in itself when it's service rendered to God. Paul writes in another place, "Whatever you do, work at it with all your heart, as working for the Lord, not for men since you know that you will receive an inheritance from the Lord as a reward. It is the Lord Christ you are serving" (Colossians 3:23–24).

In all our work we work for our Lord, and no service rendered to him is trivial. He sees our labor and it matters to him.

That perspective gives significance to everything we do, even the work we think no one notices or appreciates. Michelangelo, painting in some dark corner of the Sistine ceiling was asked by his helper why he was investing so much time and effort on a part of the painting that no one would ever see. He replied, "God will see!"

Cain

THE WAY OF CAIN

To rail is the sad privilege of the loser.

—C. S. Lewis

Writing about self-discipline in *The Book of Virtues*, William J. Bennett says, "There is much unhappiness and personal distress in the world because of failure to control [one's] temper. . . . 'Oh, if only I had stopped myself,' is an all too familiar refrain."

As a case in point, consider Cain.

In the beginning

Adam lay with his wife Eve, and she became pregnant and gave birth to Cain. She said, "With the help of the LORD I have brought forth a man." Later she gave birth to his brother Abel.

Now Abel kept flocks, and Cain worked the soil. In the course of time Cain brought some of the fruits of the soil as an offering to the LORD. But Abel brought fat portions from some of the firstborn of his flock. The LORD looked with favor on Abel and his offering, but on Cain and his offering he did not look with favor. So Cain was very angry, and his face was downcast.

Then the LORD said to Cain, "Why are you angry? Why is your face downcast? If you do what is right, will you not be accepted? But if you do not do what is right, sin is crouching at your door; it desires to have you, but you must master it."

Now Cain said to his brother Abel, "Let's go out to the field." And while they were in the field, Cain attacked his brother Abel and killed him.

Then the LORD said to Cain, "Where is your brother Abel?"

"I don't know," he replied. "Am I my brother's keeper?" (Genesis 4:1–9).

Cain's mother mistook him for the promised Messiah, a common mistake among first-time mothers. She named him Cain ("brought forth") because, she said, "with the help of the Lord, I have brought forth a man." The phrase "with the help of" added by most translations is one word in Hebrew. What Eve actually said was this: "I have brought forth a man—Yahweh.")

Eve connected the birth of her son with the fulfillment of the promise concerning the God-man who was to come (Genesis 3:15). But Cain was not the solution to the problem of sin; he was a heavy contributor to it, a chip off the old block, a son of sinful Adam. This is undoubtedly why Eve gave her second son, Abel, a more reasonable name. Abel means "breath." He was a lightweight—just breath and britches, as my mother used to say.

"Now Abel kept flocks," we're told, "and Cain worked the soil. In the course of time Cain brought some of the fruits of the soil as an offering to the LORD. But Abel brought fat portions from some of the firstborn of his flock. The LORD looked with favor on Abel and his offering, but on Cain and his offering he did not look with favor." Cain got mad and his face fell—an ancient idiom for falling into a funk.

John Milton refers to Cain as that "sweaty Reaper" who offered the hard work of his own hands to God. Abel, on the other hand, brought a suitable sacrifice: a lamb as a substitute for his sin.

The author of Hebrews suggests that the offerings went on for a while and that both were expressions of each man's heart (Hebrews 11:4). Moses picks up that emphasis stating, "The LORD looked with favor on *Abel* and his offering, but on *Cain* and his offering he did not look with favor" (Genesis 4:4–5). The problem was not the ritual; it was a matter of the heart.

The New Testament writers supply additional insight into Cain's character. The apostle John said he was a pawn of the devil: "This is the message you heard from the beginning: We should love one another. Do not be like Cain, who belonged to the evil one" (1 John 3:11–12).

Jude identified him with angry rebels everywhere who "have taken the way of Cain" (Jude 1:11).

Cain's anger at his brother grew, gnawing at him, drawing him into bitter resentment and dreary depression. God warned Cain of the consequences of his repressed fury and pointed out his only escape: "If you do what is right, will you not be accepted?" he asked. "But if you do not do what is right, sin is crouching at your door; it desires to have you, but you must master it" (Genesis 4:7). "Your anger," God seemed to say, "is like a wild beast crouching at your door, waiting to spring. You must master it or you will be mastered!"

But Cain would have none of it. He let his resentment fester, and in lethal rage he "attacked his brother Abel and killed him"—an act of aggression all the more monstrous because it was his brother he slew—and then, in cold, lingering resentment, he shrugged off his guilt: "Am I my brother's keeper?" Cain quipped.

Lethal rage

Rage can kill. It's a simple fact that most murders are not premeditated acts of violence, but "crimes of passion," committed in moments of uncontrolled frenzy, and deeply regretted after the fact.

Anger can have other deadly consequences. It can turn us into brutal abusers. It's estimated that more than half the women in America have been roughed up at least once by their husbands, and, according to the National Coalition Against Domestic Violence, three to four million women are routinely battered by their mates each year.

Civil, reasonable gentlemen can suddenly resort to brutal violence. It happens every day. Even the gentle counselor, Paul Tournier admitted: "I have on occasion slapped my wife, and have often spoken to her in the most wounding terms. I might try to reassure myself with the thought that it was only a passing accident, a mental aberration, when I was no longer myself in the heat of the moment—something soon put right! It would be more honest to say to myself that it was I who did it, and to see that it reveals an aspect of myself that I find hard to recognize; that I am much more violent than I care to acknowledge" (from *The Violence Within*).

But even if anger does not develop into physical assault, wounding tones and words can crush the soul. We chanted as children, "Sticks and stones may break my bones, but words can never hurt me," but we were denying our pain. Of course words hurt.

David speaks of those "whose tongues are sharp swords" (Psalm 57:4), suggesting the cutting, ripping effect of another's words. When we air our anger we inflict harm—sometimes irreparably—on others. We say things we never meant to say; we leave open wounds and unforgettable pain. "As long as anger lives," wrote St. John Climacus, "she continues to be the fruitful mother of many unhappy children."

And finally, though we relish anger for a while, in time truth comes in. In the end we have diminished ourselves. We have become the victims of our own rage.

Frederick Buechner writes, "Of the seven deadly sins, anger is possibly the most fun. To lick your wounds, to smack your lips over grievances long past, to roll over your tongue the prospect of bitter confrontations still to come, to savor to the last toothsome morsel both the pain you are given and the pain you are giving back . . . . The chief drawback is that what you are wolfing down is yourself. The skeleton at the feast is you" (from *Wishful Thinking: A Theological ABC*).

Different kinds of anger

Not all anger is sin. God gets angry (Hebrews 3:11); Jesus got angry (Mark 3:5); and there are occasions when we ought to be angry.

Scripture commends righteous indignation. When we hear of hideous cruelty, when others are defrauded, affronted, or insulted, we ought to be outraged.

Henry Ward Beecher said, "A man that does not know how to be angry does not know how to be good. A man that does not know how to be shaken to his heart's core with indignation over things evil is either a fungus or a wicked man."

Paul warns us, however, against indignation's tendency to develop into bitter resentment: "In your anger do not sin," he writes, "Do not let the sun go down while you are still angry" (Ephesians 4:26).

> *Anger in its time and place*
> *May assume a kind of grace.*

It must have some reason to it
And not last beyond a minute.
If to further lengths it go,
Into malice it doth grow.

—Charles and Mary Lamb[1]

Rage and resentment

Indignation, put to its intended use, is commendable. Rage and resentment are not.

Rage is uncontrolled, violent fury. Paul writes, "Get rid of bitterness, rage and anger" (Ephesians 4:31); and he cites "fits of rage" as the product of our sinful humanity (Galatians 5:20).

Resentment is rage gone underground. (Resentment is the common expression of rage for those who view outbursts of anger as sin.) Both rage and resentment are guided by selfishness and the desire to rid ourselves of those who get in our way.

William Blake wrote of his bitter resentment in a poem entitled "The Poison Tree." It describes his polite restraint while he still harbors repressed anger. His anger grows in his head like a tree, and he nurtures it until his enemy lies dead:

I was angry with my friend;
I told my wrath, my wrath did end.
I was angry with my foe;
I told it not, my wrath did grow.

And I watered it with fears,
Night and morning with my tears,
And I sunned it with smiles
And with soft deceitful wiles.

---

[1]The irony of this poem is that Mary Lamb herself, in a moment of insane rage, murdered her own mother.

And it grew both day and night,
Till it bore an apple bright,
And my foe beheld it shine,
And he knew that it was mine—

And into my garden stole
When the night had veiled the pole:
In the morning, glad, I see
My foe outstretched beneath the tree.

Causes of anger

Anger is a "blanket emotion" that covers an array of other feelings and affections. When our sense of security is imperiled, when we lose power in a relationship, when our imperfections are revealed, when we are rejected, we feel frustrated and angry.

Bottom line, anger is the response we make to outraged love: "The fluid that love bleeds when you cut it," as C. S. Lewis said. What we want is boundless love. When we are frustrated in that pursuit we feel threatened and are propelled into action. We want to fight back.

Threatening situations cause our nervous system to kick in, activating our adrenal glands to secrete chemicals which in turn stimulate a number of organs in our bodies to prepare us to resist and fight. That chemical reaction is what gives us that hard-to-describe feeling of arousal we call anger.

There's nothing sinful about angry feelings. They are an indispensable expression of the natural defense system with which God has equipped us. But when we permit these feelings to push us over the edge, when we give way to blind rage, we demean others, we debase ourselves, and, more important, we dishonor the God in whose image we are created.

Can anger be controlled?

We tend to think of anger as an instinctive, reflexive, unconscious, biological reaction beyond our control. Must we then hold ourselves responsible?

We must. The Bible condemns inappropriate expressions of anger and commends those who keep anger under control. The wise man says,

> Better a patient man [one slow to anger] than a warrior, a man who controls his temper than one who takes a city (Proverbs 16:32).

> A fool gives full vent to his anger, but a wise man keeps himself under control (Proverbs 29:11).

Four components

Recent studies on anger support what the Bible has been saying all along: *Anger can be controlled and sanctified through truth.* Let me explain.

Anger involves four components: (1) the activating experience (a crying baby, a tardy spouse, a thoughtless remark); (2) an inner emotional reaction to the threat; (3) a series of thoughts that either augment or mitigate the anger; and (4) an outer behavioral response.

These components are so intertwined that we experience them as one continuous surge. That's why we tend to think of anger as an emotion beyond our control. We lose hope for change because we lose sight of the thinking and behaving components of anger and focus on the physiological surge of emotional arousal.

But the behavioral response is governed by our ways of thinking about ourselves and about the person who is making us angry. The intensity of our anger is based on those thoughts. We reach the stage of towering rage because we permit our thoughts to drive us to it.

What I am saying is this: *What we think before, during, and after the initial surge of anger determines our outward behavior.*

This is nothing new. The Bible makes it clear that any progress toward godliness is the result of proper thinking. Our thought life is the key element in emotional and behavioral control, and that control grows as we acquire additional truth on which to set our minds. We are what we *think*, Jesus insists (Matthew 12:35).

Doing what is right

James puts all of this together and provides the key:

My dear brothers, take note of this: Everyone should be quick to listen, slow to speak and slow to become angry, for man's anger does not bring about the righteous life that God desires (1:19–20).

These are the steps James envisions:

1. Acknowledge your anger

It's good to say, "I am getting angry"—to ourselves or to the person with whom we are angry.

It's hard for some people to accept their anger because they falsely equate it with sin, but no emotion is evil in itself. Emotions can only incline us to evil.

2. Hold back your anger

The next step is to be "slow to become angry." In the words of an old slogan, "The only time to procrastinate is when you're angry."

We can and must hold back our anger for a time. This is not repression (holding anger in), but rather a matter of slowing down the rapid escalation of emotion, perhaps by the time-honored expedient of taking a few deep breaths and trying to relax our muscles or counting to ten.

Plutarch, the Roman playwright, had one of his characters say to the emperor, "Remember, Caesar, whenever you are angry, say or do nothing until you have repeated the four-and-twenty letters [of the alphabet] to yourself."

Or, if we feel ourselves getting out of control, we can call time out and separate ourselves temporarily from the conflict or provoking situation, giving our emotions time to subside and allowing our thinking processes time to emerge. A little time out will help us "get our minds right," as Cool Hand Luke would say.

The main thing is to retard our anger and give ourselves time to think. "Anger is the anesthetic of the mind," C. S. Lewis said. Once a certain point is reached rationality goes out the window. It's important to slow our thought processes down and begin to analyze how we're thinking.

3. Be slow to speak

Literally. Speak slowly or not at all.

John Henry, Cardinal Newman said, "There is in stillness oft a magic power/To calm the breast when struggling passions lower." Restraining our tongues has the effect of slowing down our thought processes so we can begin to think clearly, rationally, and analytically. Speak when angry and we inevitably make the best speech we ever regretted.

4. Be quick to listen

And then we should *listen*—listen to what *God* has to say and think his thoughts after him. That's what James means by being "quick to listen."

Note the context: "He chose to give us birth through the *word of truth*, that we might be a kind of first fruits of all he created. My dear brothers, take note of this: Everyone should be quick to *listen*, slow to speak and slow to become angry (James 1:18–19).

Listen to what? Listen to the "word of truth," an idea he elaborates in verse 22: "Do not merely listen to the word, and so deceive yourselves. Do what it says."

What we must do is slow our thinking down and mentally challenge our thoughts—correct the lies that inform our thoughts and replace them with truth.

Our erroneous zones

All of us have erroneous beliefs about life: We believe against all evidence to the contrary that everything should go our way: our children should always behave; our opinions should always be considered; our spouses and friends should always be reasonable, cheerful, helpful, and kind; others should always listen to us, understand us and do our bidding. In short, everyone ought to love us all the time under all conditions of life.

According to psychologist Albert Ellis, the most common mental aberrations are these:

I must always win the approval of others for my performances, or else I am a rotten person.

Others must treat me considerately and kindly and in precisely the way I want them to treat me.

The world (and the people in it) must arrange the conditions under which I live so that I get everything I want when I want it.

That's a pack of lies. We should listen to God's voice and challenge our self-pity, discouragement, and jealousy and replace them with truth:

I live in a broken world with broken people who will frequently break my heart. Nevertheless, I am deeply loved by God.

It's up to God to give me what I need, when he thinks I need it. In the meantime, I am steadfastly kept in his care.

When truth comes in, the lies that have informed our thinking slowly begin to lose their force and our anger begins to abate.

James continues

James completes his argument in chapter 4 where he explains the reason for fights and quarrels:

> What causes fights and quarrels among you? Don't they come from your desires that battle within you? You want something but don't get it. You kill and covet, but you cannot have what you want. You quarrel and fight. You do not have, because you do not ask God (James 4:1–2).

James swings his ax at the root of our problem: we're hedonists at heart. (The Greek word from which the translation "desires" is taken is the word from which we get our word *hedonism.*) We want to be pleasured, and when we don't get what we want, we go to war!

It's that smothering absorption with getting our way and having our needs met—being acknowledged, understood, cared for, catered to, listened to—that brings us into conflict with others. People don't come through for us and that makes us angry, an anger that quickly becomes blind rage, cruelty, and force.

The answer, according to James, is to give up the ruthless pursuit of our pleasure and ask God to supply what we desire in his own time and in his own way and to ask with our wills resigned: "Not my will but yours be done."

Bernard of Clairvaux wrote long ago, "What will you do if your needs are not met? Will you look to God to meet your needs? God promises that those who seek first the kingdom and his righteousness will have all things added to them. God promises that to those who restrict themselves and give to their neighbor he will give whatever is necessary. Seeking first the kingdom means to prefer to bear the yoke of modesty (humility) and restraint rather than allow sin to reign in your mortal body" (from *On the Love of God*).

Asking God to meet our needs is a better way than our way (and Cain's way) for, as James says, when God meets our needs he gives a "greater grace" (4:6)—a sense of well-being far greater than anything we can get on our own.

Making progress

Growth takes time. We must be patient with God while he brings it about. As we learn truth we will begin to develop a mind-set that will reduce our emotional reactions to threat. As our hearts become increasingly convinced that God loves us unconditionally and wants to meet our needs, we will find ourselves less inclined to react emotionally to indifference, criticism, or rebuke.

A secure person is less likely to have an adrenaline surge when a client complains about her performance. The person who realizes that God is sovereign and controls all the details of life is less likely to get angry at 5:00 p.m. traffic. Men and women who know they are in God's grip can be patient and calm in the face of terror and intimidation.

This is the maturity "from which foundation we are more prepared for the loving confrontation required in all relationships and the righteous indignation required in a fallen world. Learning to be slow to anger gives us the time and freedom of mind to decide how we should solve our problems or how we should express our anger. Being slow to anger allows us to respond to conviction, to confess our sins of anger and to rise above hate to forgive those who have offended us. From this foundation of holding anger back are made the decisions for how and when to express anger, for anger problems are not fully resolved simply because people hold back. Relationship problems in particular demand the proper expression of anger and the consequent resolution of problems" (Mark P. Cosgrove in *Counseling for Anger*).

No final failure

Of course we will fail. Whoever thought otherwise? But no failure is final. God is a God of an infinite number of chances.

Leonardo da Vinci was working on his painting "The Last Supper" one afternoon when something one of his assistants did angered him. Losing his temper, he lashed the other fellow with bitter words.

Leonardo returned to his canvas and went to work on the nearly completed portrait of Jesus, but he could not go on.

Looking into the calm and patient face of Jesus, as he himself had envisioned him, Leonardo was reminded of his own tantrum and thoughtless words. Putting down his tools, he sought out the subject of his wrath and asked for forgiveness. Then he went back to his work of making Christ known.

We will fall; as C. S. Lewis pointed out, we will be very dirty children by the time we get home. The only fatal thing is to give up.

Some proverbs to ponder . . .

A fool shows his annoyance at once, but a prudent man overlooks an insult (12:16).

When we retaliate we only make things worse—add injury to insult. It's better to let the insult go by.

A quick-tempered man does foolish things, and a crafty man is hated (14:17).

Another version of the proverb, "Fools rush in . . . ."

*A patient man has great understanding, but a
quick-tempered man displays folly (14:29).*

To see calmly is to see clearly.

*A gentle answer turns away wrath, but a harsh
word stirs up anger (15:1).*

An angry retort only mobilizes another's defenses.
Don't fuel anger; quench it with a quiet word.

*A hot-tempered man stirs up dissension, but a
patient man calms a quarrel (15:18).*

Patience calms people down. It is the environment in
which quarrels die a natural death.

*Better a patient man than a warrior, a man who
controls his temper than one who takes a city (16:32).*

As a friend of mine restated this proverb, "A calm
man is more macho than an angry man."

*A man's wisdom gives him patience; it is to his
glory to overlook an offense (19:11).*

The secret to anger management is managing our
minds.

*Do not make friends with a hot-tempered man, do
not associate with one easily angered (22:24).*

We learn to be angry by being around angry people.
"Evil companions corrupt good manners," Paul says.

A fool gives full vent to his anger [Hebrew: "lets his spirit go out"], but a wise man keeps himself under control (29:11).

Anger management is not repression but the discipline of wisdom.

An angry person stirs up dissension, and a hot-tempered one commits many sins (29:22).

I think of Moses and the incident at Meribah: "By the waters of Meribah they angered the LORD, and trouble came to Moses" (Psalm 106:32). See also Ephesians 4:26–30.

For as churning the milk produces butter, and as twisting the nose produces blood, so stirring up anger produces strife (30:33).

There's "a time to hold 'em and a time to fold 'em and a time to walk away." If you find yourself getting angry and out of control, call time-out.

By three things a man is known . . .

his *cûs* (his behavior when drinking);
his *cîs* (the way he handles his money)
his *ca'as* (his temper)

—from the Babylonian Talmud

Jehoshaphat

FACING OUR FEARS

We become brave by doing brave acts.

—Aristotle

Marine Corps General Chesty Puller once referred to the Korean Conflict as a "dirty little war, but the only one we have." I was in the military then and, though I never saw combat in Korea, I saw some of the casualties of that dirty little war. It was an engagement in which the enemy refused to fight fair.

I've seen the look of terror in men's eyes, unfaded by years of relative safety—the look of men who've been to hell and back and can't forget what they've seen.

I've seen that same terrible look in the eyes of men who've told me they have prostate cancer, are victims of corporate downsizing, are facing bankruptcy and ruin, or have been abandoned by their wives. They too look as though they've been to hell and back; they too have seen an enemy that will not fight fair.

There is an irony about anxiety, however, that takes away its power: it can make us braver than we ever were before. Courage is not fearlessness, but a settled disposition to do what is right in the face of our fear. "Courage is not the absence of fear," reads a line in *The Red Badge of Courage,* "it is the ability to do what we must."

There's a narrative in the Old Testament that makes that point. It's the story of King Jehoshaphat, a man who learned to face down his fears.

A day in the life of Jehoshaphat

Jehoshaphat was a relatively obscure ruler of the southern kingdom of Judah. Second Chronicles 20 reports on a day in his life that began like any other day, but quickly turned into chaos:

> After this, the Moabites and Ammonites with some of the Meunites came to make war on Jehoshaphat.
> Some men came and told Jehoshaphat, "A vast army is coming against you from Edom, from the other side of the Sea. It is already in Hazazon Tamar" (2 Chronicles 20:1–2).

It was "after this," our author notes, that enemies from the east sought to invade and overcome Judah. It is significant that these armies massed and mounted their attack at this particular time. Jehoshaphat was on a high. This was a time of great victory for the young king. God had made him his instrument to bring about a great revival (2 Chron-icles 19:4–11).

With the announcement of the invasion King Jehoshaphat came down from his high in a hurry. Hazazon Tamar was only fifteen miles from Jerusalem, less than a day's march away.

This was a daring and unexpected move in which the invaders crossed the Dead Sea, probably at a ford opposite

Masada, and climbed one of the difficult assents directly into the heart of the Judean hills. Before Jehoshaphat was aware of their presence they were in position to strike Jerusalem, the capital city of Judah. The crisis was total!

Crises come like this, unbidden, unexpected, and often after some life-changing decision or a period of spiritual gain. We should expect them: every advance on our part will always be met by a counterattack from the far side. The question is not, Will we be assaulted? The questions are, When will we be attacked? and What shall we do when it happens?

Jehoshaphat knew what to do:

> Alarmed, Jehoshaphat resolved to inquire of the
> LORD, and he proclaimed a fast for all Judah. The
> people of Judah came together to seek help from the
> LORD; indeed, they came from every town in Judah to
> seek him (2 Chronicles 20:3–4).

Jehoshaphat was badly frightened, and he admitted it—unlike some men who deny their fear. It's too bad that they do, because the first step to overcoming any anxiety is to face it. The current "no fear" fad is pure baloney. A man who does not know fear is unsafe and unsound, a menace to himself and to others.

Fear ought to lead us to do the best thing, what Jehoshaphat did. He inquired of the Lord and sought help from him. That's a reflex unknown to ordinary men, who first search their own minds for the thing to do. Jehoshaphat, an extraordinary man, stood with his people in the house of the Lord and prayed.

> Then Jehoshaphat stood up in the assembly of
> Judah and Jerusalem at the temple of the LORD in the
> front of the new courtyard and said:
> "O LORD, God of our fathers, are you not the God
> who is in heaven? You rule over all the kingdoms of the

nations. Power and might are in your hand, and no one can withstand you. O our God, did you not drive out the inhabitants of this land before your people Israel and give it for ever to the descendants of Abraham your friend? They have lived in it and have built in it a sanctuary for your Name, saying, 'If calamity comes upon us, whether the sword of judgment, or plague or famine, we will stand in your presence before this temple that bears your Name and will cry out to you in our distress, and you will hear us and save us.'

"But now here are men from Ammon, Moab and Mount Seir, whose territory you would not allow Israel to invade when they came from Egypt; so they turned away from them and did not destroy them. See how they are repaying us by coming to drive us out of the possession you gave us as an inheritance. O our God, will you not judge them? For we have no power to face this vast army that is attacking us. We do not know what to do, but our eyes are upon you."

All the men of Judah, with their wives and children and little ones, stood there before the LORD (2 Chronicles 20:5–13).

Jehoshaphat focused first on God and found that everything was under control in heaven and earth. At ground-level the view was appalling, but there was no panic above. Like John he saw the Lord on his throne resting on a "sea of glass." There was no fuss, no frenzy, no hysteria.

God was not pacing the floor, biting his nails, wondering what in the world he would do. He always knows what to do. He always "works out everything in conformity with the purpose of his will" (Ephesians 1:11). There's no need to worry.

"God works in tranquillity," one old saint has said. And those who know the God of peace share his calm and quiet nature.

God is working out his purpose
    'spite of all that happens here
Lawless nations in commotion,
    restless like a storm-tossed ocean
He controls their rage and fury
    so his children need not fear.
Let our hearts then turn to heaven
    where he bides his time in peace
Giving him our heart's devotion
    till the present troubles cease.

—Author unknown

Then Jehoshaphat looked back and thought about God's faithfulness in the past: "O our God, did you not drive out the inhabitants of this land before your people Israel and give it forever to the descendants of Abraham, your friend?" (20:7).

He reminded himself that God had given Canaan to his people by covenant; he had guaranteed their integrity in the land. No one could oust them without his permission.

Those who had lived when God gave Israel land, and had learned their faith back then, said that when crises came, a man could cry out to God in his distress and he would be heard and saved (20:9). And so Jehoshaphat prayed: "Now, here they are—men from Ammon, Moab and Mount Seir. . . . O our God will you not judge them? For we have no power to face this vast army that is attacking us. We do not know what to do but our eyes are on you" (20:10–12).

There is a significant juxtaposition of two thoughts here: "Power and might are in your hand . . ." (20:6), and, "We have no power . . ." (20:12).

We have no power; God has it all. He does not give power to anyone in the sense that his power is ours to have and to hold. We are *always* weak. We are *never* strong. The only strength we have is the strength that comes from God. "Not that we are sufficient in ourselves," Paul echoes, "but our sufficiency is from God" (2 Corinthians 3:5).

Sometimes we feel weak; sometimes we feel strong. But we must always keep in mind that we are never strong, even when we feel that way. We are *always* needy, *always* incompetent, *always* inadequate, *always* inept, *always* desperately dependent on God. Without him we can do *nothing*.

Perhaps the most startling of all Jesus' statements about himself was his insistence that he too was an inadequate being. "The Son," he said, "can do *nothing* of himself" (John 5:30).

Jesus' incarnation included taking on our weakness. He, like us, had to rely on God every moment of every day. Each morning he had to abandon his own strength and strategies and offer himself up, confident that his Father's power would lead him into greater works than he could envision or accomplish alone. "Oh the mystery of humility," F. B. Meyer said, "that he who planned all things should live a life of such absolute dependence."

I recall walking into Ray Stedman's office one day to lament my own limitations. Some months before, I had been handed a large ministry. I knew I would surely fail. "I'm so inadequate," I bemoaned.

"Yes, you are, my friend—and so am I," Ray quipped, "and it's good that we know it. Some men labor all their lives never knowing that they're inadequate."

Jehoshaphat knew. He looked at his limitations and then looked to the Lord as the only source of his help: "We do not know what to do, but our eyes are upon *you*." That's a prayer we should breathe every moment of every day, not just when our backs are against the wall. When that becomes our mindset then significant things begin to happen.

G. K. Chesterton once pointed out that if a man needs wisdom, he may cry out, "William Shakespeare, help me!" and nothing much will happen. If he needs courage, he may cry out, "Billy Budd, help me! and nothing much will happen. But for two thousand years, whenever a man has cried out, "Lord Jesus, help me," something truly momentous happens.

Something happened after Jehoshaphat's plea. Someone in the crowd spoke up—Jahaziel, one of the brothers:

> "Listen, King Jehoshaphat and all who live in Judah
> and Jerusalem! This is what the LORD says to you:
> 'Do not be afraid or discouraged because of this vast
> army. For the battle is not yours, but God's.
> Tomorrow march down against them. . . . You will not
> have to fight this battle. Take up your positions; stand
> firm and see the deliverance the LORD will give you
> . . . . Do not be afraid; do not be discouraged. Go out
> to face them tomorrow, and the LORD will be with
> you' " (20:15–18).

The battle was the Lord's. It was his business to do the fighting. Jehoshaphat's role was to stand fast and see what God would do. This is what Paul means when he writes,

> Be strong in the Lord and in his mighty power. Put on
> the full armor of God so that you can take your stand
> against the devil's schemes. . . . Therefore put on the
> full armor of God, so that when the day of evil comes,
> you may be able to stand your ground, and after you
> have done everything, to stand (Ephesians 6:10–13).

"Standing" is a mental posture, a refusal to run away, to retreat into self-indulgent and self-protective devices. It is a matter of standing one's ground and waiting to see what God will do.

But standing also means engaging our fears. We have to "march down against them"; we must identify the thing we fear and face it. That's sometimes the hardest thing in the world to do. Our natural inclination is to flee.

John Bunyan, in *The Pilgrim's Progress,* tells how Christian encountered Apollyon, the hideous, scaled monster who blocked his progress to the Celestial City. Apollyon taunted him and tried to intimidate him, and he almost succeeded: "Christian began to be afraid, and to cast in his mind whether to go back, or to stand his ground. But he considered again, that he had no armor for his back, and therefore thought that to turn the back to him might give him greater advantage with ease to pierce him with his darts." So Christian resolved to face the fiend because, he said, "it is the only way to stand."

We must not run from our fears; we only expose ourselves to greater danger when we do. We must "get in the face" of those things we fear and then see what God will do.

The next day

The next morning Jehoshaphat's fears returned, as they always do, but he looked again into God's Word and found there the assurance he needed to go on. He said to his army, "Have faith in the LORD your God and you will be upheld; have faith in the prophets and you will be successful" (20:20). Faith comes by hearing and hearing by the Word of God.

This is what Paul means when he writes,

> Take up the shield of faith, with which you can
> extinguish all the flaming arrows of the evil one. Take
> the helmet of salvation and the sword of the Spirit,
> which is the word of God (Ephesians 6:16–17).

Satan never gives up. He continues to harass us, reminding us of our impotence and inability to act, insinuating that God cannot be trusted to keep his word. "Has God really said . . . ?" he sneers.

He flings himself against us again and again. He tries to overwhelm us with repeated assaults. For each attack we must raise the shield of faith and unsheathe our sword—stir ourselves to remember what God has said and get a good grip on his word.

Once again, Bunyan's description of Christian's encounter with Apollyon helps us understand the process. Apollyon, unable to dissuade Christian from his journey, turned from subtlety to brutality: he hurled a flaming spear at Christian's breast. But the good man deflected it with his shield.

> Then did Christian draw his sword, for he saw 'twas time to bestir him; and Apollyon as fast made at him, throwing darts as thick as hail; by the which, notwithstanding all that Christian could do to avoid it, Apollyon wounded him in his head, his hand, and foot. This made Christian give a little back; Apollyon, therefore, followed his work amain, and Christian again took courage, and resisted as manfully as he could. This sore combat lasted for above half a day, even till Christian was almost quite spent. For you must know that Christian, by reason of his wounds, must needs grow weaker and weaker.
>
> Then Apollyon, espying his opportunity, began to gather up close to Christian, and wrestling with him gave him a dreadful fall; and with that Christian's sword flew out of his hand. Then said Apollyon, "I am sure of thee now!" And with that, he had almost pressed him to death, so that Christian began to despair of life. But as God would have it, while Apollyon was fetching of his last blow, thereby to make a full end of this good man, Christian nimbly reached out his hand for his sword, and caught it, saying, "Rejoice not against me, O mine enemy! When I fall, I shall arise" [Micah 7:8]; and with that gave him a deadly thrust, which made him give back, as one that had received his mortal wound. Christian

perceiving that, made at him again, saying, "Nay, in
all these things we are more than conquerors, through
him that loved us" [Romans 8:37]. And with that
Apollyon spread forth his dragon's wings, and sped
him away. And Christian saw him no more.

So then, with confidence restored, Jehoshaphat marched
off to face his foes. The band struck up a tune, and
Jehoshaphat and his army went off to war, singing an old
sustaining song: "Give thanks to the LORD, for he is good. His
love endures forever."

Imagine the march. Jehoshaphat reached the top of the
first hill from which he could look down into the Jordan
valley. There he saw his enemies massing for the attack. Then
they were lost from sight as he dropped into a valley.

He climbed another hill from which he could look down
on the Ascent of Ziz and see the enemy on the march up the
wadi. He descended and once again his enemies disappeared
from view only to appear again at the next rise. Each hill
became another occasion to renew his faith.

Then as he approached the final hilltop he drew his sword
and led the charge—to find "only dead bodies on the ground"
(2 Chronicles 20:22–24). "The LORD had set ambushes
against the men of Ammon and Moab and Mount Seir who
were invading Judah, and they were defeated. The men of
Ammon and Moab rose up against the men from Mount Seir
to destroy and annihilate them. After they finished
slaughtering the men from Seir, they helped to destroy one
another."

Jehoshaphat's enemies were DOA. There was nothing left
of them but their booty.

So Jehoshaphat and his men went to carry off their
plunder, and they found among them a great amount
of equipment and clothing and also articles of value—

more than they could take away. There was so much plunder that it took three days to collect it.

There's an old saying: "To a crow in the know a scarecrow is an invitation to a feast." Jehoshaphat and his army plundered their adversaries and returned with the spoils of war. Is this not what Paul means when he says we are "more than conquerors through him who loved us"? God takes the very thing we fear and turns it to ringing triumph.

On the march

This assault upon Judah is suggestive to me of those unexpected crises we experience that come out of nowhere, often at a time when things are going especially well.

When we least expect it, a messenger arrives at our house with a registered letter from a lawyer; a summons comes from the IRS; a warrant is served for our son's arrest; our doctor leaves a call informing us that our lab tests look bad and something is terribly wrong. And our hearts begin to pound.

The fear we experience at such times is perfectly normal. It is not cowardice. It is a natural, instinctive reaction to a situation beyond our control.

I'm personally afraid of men who are fearless. Starbuck, the chief mate of Captain Ahab's boat *The Pequod,* said, "I will have no man in my boat who is not afraid of a whale." I agree. I don't drift our Idaho rivers with men who have no fear, and I don't fly with bush pilots who aren't afraid. There are old pilots and bold pilots, as they say, but there are no old, bold pilots. There are some things a man ought to be afraid of. If he isn't, there's something wrong with him.

The problem is not fear, but our response to it. Jesus often said to his disciples, "fear not," but the tense he employed referred not to their immediate response to danger, but to *persistent* fear—fear that paralyzes and hinders them from doing what they knew they ought to do.

Though I rarely agree with theologian Paul Tillich, I think he had the right idea when he argued that courage is the foundation of virtue. Fear is what prevents obedience.

Fear is not sin, but disobedience is, and fear can lead to disobedience. We listen to our racing pulses and ringing ears and react in ungodly ways. We lash out at our colleagues, our wife and children, and God. We deny our fear and cover up with bravado or we flee from it into alcohol and drugs. We resort to scheming on our own and make decisions that exclude God's wisdom. As a consequence we never find out what God can do.

We should rather seek God's face and that tranquil place where he dwells. There's no panic there. In that quiet place we must read and reflect on his word and find out what he wants us to do. He will supply the wisdom that we need.

And then we must sally forth in faith to face the thing we fear, singing to ourselves about our Lord's love, thanking him for a victory already won, believing that the battle is not ours but the Lord's.

He will do all the rest. He will either do away with our enemies or he will take us through the encounter unscathed. He will deliver us from evil and surprise us with joy. The valley we have dreaded will have become a valley of blessing forevermore (2 Chronicles 20:26).

The prophet Joel, when speaking about the coming of our Lord, calls the place of his final conflict "The Valley of Jehoshaphat" (Joel 3:2, 12). Jehoshaphat's victory in his day was symbolic of all God's victories and finds its final application in the ultimate defeat of all the enemies of our soul.

In the meantime, every dark and dangerous valley can be the Valley of Jehoshaphat—the place where God puts to death our fears.

"The Lord shall fight for you, and you
shall hold your peace."
Look up, O you of little faith;
let doubting cease.

The battle is the Lord's; He works
in a mysterious way.
'Tis not by might, nor power, but see
His spirit move today.

Unprofitable servants we;
our duty done, we must
watch for his victory,
so, fearful one, be still and trust.

—Ruth Bell Graham

David

THE DISCIPLINE
OF DISGRACE

*The only wisdom we can hope to acquire
is the wisdom of humility; humility is endless.*

—T. S. Eliot

Just about the time I think I've got it all together, some unsightly emotional display, some inappropriate reaction, some other embarrassing behavior blows my cover and I have that horrible experience of being found out. It's humiliating!

But humiliation is good for the soul. Through it God deals with our self-admiration and pride. Without it we could never make the most of our lives.

The trouble with us is that we want to be tremendously important. It's a terrible trait, the essential vice, the utmost evil. It's the sin that turned the devil into the demon he became.

Obscurity and humility, on the other hand, release God's greatness. It is the basis of our life with God and our usefulness in this world. Thomas à Kempis wrote, "The more humble a man is in himself, and the more subject unto God; so much more prudent shall he be in all his affairs, and enjoy greater peace and quietness of heart."

Because ambition and pride is the center of our resistance to God and the source of so much unhappiness, "God opposes the proud" (James 4:6); he brings us to our knees, where He can then begin to do something with us.

Here's another story about David and how God worked through the most humiliating experience of his life:

> David fled from Saul and went to Achish king of Gath. But the servants of Achish said to him, "Isn't this David, the king of the land? Isn't he the one they sing about in their dances: 'Saul has slain his thousands, and David his tens of thousands'?"
>
> David took these words to heart and was very much afraid of Achish king of Gath. So he pretended to be insane in their presence; and while he was in their hands he acted like a madman, making marks on the doors of the gate and letting saliva run down his beard.
>
> Achish said to his servants, "Look at the man! He is insane! Why bring him to me? Am I so short of madmen that you have to bring this fellow here to carry on like this in front of me? Must this [mad] man come into my house?"
>
> David [then] left Gath and escaped to the cave of Adullam (1 Samuel 21:10–22:1).

David fled south from Nob—with Saul in hot pursuit—and he made his way across the Judean hills and through the Valley of Elah where a few years before he had engaged Goliath in combat.

Ten miles away, further down the valley, lay Gath. Gath was one of the five cities of the Philistines (Gaza, Ashdod, Ashkelon, Ekron, Gath), all located on or near the southern coast of Palestine in the region now known as the Gaza Strip. It was the city from which Goliath had been sent out to the Valley of Elah to challenge Israel. It was to Gath—the home of his enemies—that David now turned for shelter from Saul.

I don't know what possessed David to flee to Gath. Perhaps he thought he wouldn't be recognized, since this was several years after his encounter with Goliath, and he had grown to manhood. Perhaps he disguised himself in some way. But David was instantly recognized, and his presence was reported to king Achish of Gath: "Isn't this David, the king of the land? Isn't he the one they sing about in their dances: 'Saul has slain his thousands, and David his tens of thousands'?"

The phrase "they sing" could be translated, "they *still* sing," suggesting a popular tune. David's fame was celebrated everywhere—even in Philistia.

You have to understand the implications of this song. David had slain his ten thousands of *Philistines*; his fame had been established at the expense of bereaved Philistine women and children. Here was an opportunity to take vengeance.

Furthermore, he was considered "the king of the land [of Israel]." It's doubtful that the Philistines knew of David's divine election and secret anointing, but they must have thought of David as the *defacto* king of Israel.

By some means David became aware that he had been found out, and that he was facing imprisonment and death, so David lost his nerve (see Psalm 34 and 56). Motivated by sheer terror, David pretended to go mad, foaming at the mouth and scrawling crazy slogans on the walls.

According to the title of Psalm 56 the Philistines "seized him" and brought him to Achish, who dismissed him with the contemptuous remark: "Behold, you see a madman! Why have you brought him to me? Am I lacking madmen that you have brought *this* to ply his madness against me? Must *this* come into my house?"

The word translated "mad man" (21:15), used three times by Achish, suggests something other than insanity. The word in other Near Eastern languages means "highly aggressive" —violent and dangerous—which gives added force to the king's remark: ". . . you have brought this to ply his madness [ravings] *against* me?" Achish was afraid of David. The title to Psalm 34 supplies the conclusion of the matter: Achish *"drove him away,"* out of his court and out of town—David, run out of town on a rail, utterly humiliated. David, the tough guy, the hero of Israel, the man they celebrated in song and dance had wimped out in the face of physical danger and made an utter fool of himself.

With no place else to go, unwelcome in both Israel and Philistia, David fled into a labyrinth of broken ridges and rimrock about three miles from Gath and crept into a cave.

The cavern in which he found refuge was called the Cave of Adullum (*Adullam* means refuge). It can't be located with certainty, but the traditional site is a dark vault located on a shelf at the top of a near-perpendicular cliff. In that dark place—humiliated, crushed, alone—he wrote Psalm 34 and Psalm 56. He was at his nadir.

In that dark place David cried out to God: "This poor [humiliated] man called, and the LORD heard him." There he learned that "The LORD is close to the brokenhearted and saves those who are crushed in spirit" (34:6, 18). Lord Byron wrote from Reading Jail, "How else but through a broken heart can Lord Christ enter in?"

Furthermore, David learned to boast in the Lord rather than in his own ability (34:2). Through shame and disgrace he became a more modest man—one whom God could shape and use.

The wisdom of humility

Pride is the seat of all unrighteousness and unpleasant-ness. It's what separates us from God and from one another. That's why God must oppose it.

God has many ways to bring us to our knees, but the best way is through humiliation. He brings us to the place where we see how utterly depraved we are. When we've been thoroughly shamed and broken, then God can do something with us.

John Newton knew:

> *I asked the Lord that I may grow*
> *in faith and love and every grace.*
> *Might more of his salvation know,*
> *and seek more earnestly his face.*
>
> *'Twas He who taught me thus to pray,*
> *and He I trust has answered prayer,*
> *But it has been in such a way*
> *as almost drove me to despair.*
>
> *I thought that in some favored hour,*
> *at once He'd answer my request,*
> *And by His love's transforming power,*
> *Subdue my sins and give me rest.*
>
> *Instead of that He made me see*
> *the hidden evils of my heart,*
> *And bade the angry powers of hell*
> *assault my soul in every part.*
>
> *Nay, more, with His hand He seemed*
> *intent to aggravate my woe,*
> *Crossed all the fair designs I schemed,*
> *blasted my gourds, and laid me low.*

"Lord, why this?" I trembling cried.
  "Wilt Thou pursue this worm to death?"
"This is the way," the Lord replied,
  "I answer prayer for grace and faith."

"These inward trials I employ
  from sin and self to set thee free,
And cross thy schemes of earthly joy
  that thou might find thy all in Me."

Our humiliations are not cruel accidents. They are handed to us by a gracious, kindly Father. He exposes our depravity so he can bring it to an end. Our dishonor takes us to the place where we glory in our weakness rather than in our perceived strength.

The unwise decision that wipes out our business, the thoughtless remark that makes us look like a fool, the shameful outburst that flames our face, the moral failure that impairs our reputation—these are God's gifts to us. By the time they have reached us they have been filtered through his goodness and mercy. It is the will of a Father and Friend whose wisdom and love are infinite.

God's intentions are always good. He has no other motive than love. He lets us humiliate ourselves, not to ruin us, but to lift us up higher than we've ever been before (1 Peter 5:6).

The author of Hebrews has this to say,

"My son, do not make light of the Lord's discipline,
    and do not lose heart when he rebukes you,
because the Lord disciplines those he loves,
    and he punishes everyone he accepts as a son."

Endure hardship as discipline; God is treating you as sons. For what son is not disciplined by his father? If you are not disciplined (and everyone undergoes discipline), then you are illegitimate children and not true sons. Moreover, we have all had human fathers who disciplined us and we respected them for it. How much more should we submit to the Father of our spirits and live! Our fathers disciplined us for a little while as they thought best; but God disciplines us for our good, that we may share in his holiness. No discipline seems pleasant at the time, but painful. Later on, however, it produces a harvest of righteousness and peace for those who have been trained by it (12:5–11).

Humiliation is not punishment. Jesus took that chastisement on the cross (Isaiah 53:5). There is now no condemnation (Romans 6:1). Nor does our humbling arise out of God's frustration and anger. No, he disciplines us for our good, to produce a harvest of holiness and humility. "Where grows the golden grain?" Maltbie Babcock asks. "In a furrow cut by pain."

Our response to humiliation is the test of our understanding of God's heart. Do we resist his loving discipline? Do we become resentful at it? Do we try to hide ourselves and our shame? Or are we "trained" by it? Do we see the affection behind the hand that humbles us; do we accept the burning shame and let it make us what God wants us to be?

> He said, "I will crowd action upon action,
> The strife of faction
> Shall stir me and sustain;
> O tears that drown the fire of manhood cease."
> But vain the word: vain, vain;
> Not in endeavor lieth peace.
>
> He said, "I will withdraw me and be quiet;
> Why meddle in life's riot?
> Shut be my door to pain.

Desire, thou dost fool me, thou shall cease."
But vain the word: vain, vain;
Not in aloofness lieth peace.

He said, "I will submit; I am defeated,
God hath depleted
My life of its richest gain.
O futile murmerings, why will ye not cease?"
But vain the word: vain, vain;
Not in submission lieth peace.

He said, "I will accept the breaking sorrow
Which God tomorrow
Will to his son explain."
Then did the turmoil deep within him cease.
Not vain the word: vain, vain;
For in acceptance lieth peace.

—Amy Carmichael

Dying to ourselves

William Law wrote, "Accept every [humiliation] with both your hands as a true opportunity and blessed occasion for dying to self and entering into a fuller fellowship with your self-denying, suffering Savior. Look at no inward or outward trouble with any other view. Reject every other thought about it. And then every bitterness will become the blessed day of your prosperity."

"Dying to self," as Law said, is the issue. Everything comes down to our readiness to die. Until we're willing to put to death our need to be prominent and important we will never amount to anything. Jesus said, "If anyone would come after me, he must deny himself and take up his cross daily and follow me" (Luke 9:23).

The cross in Roman times was designed for one purpose only—for dying. It had no other use. It has no other use today. It is the place where we put to death our pride and presumption and quietly humble ourselves under the mighty hand of God. "Not my will, but yours be done."

Cross-bearing is accepting humiliation and living with it while it bides its time. Rome's prisoners fought and struggled with their executioners. They refused to mount their crosses until they were lashed into submission. It must not be true of us. We must quietly and humbly accept the place where we're stretched out to die. "In acceptance lieth peace."

It is in proportion as we see God's will in our humiliation and surrender ourselves to bear it that we will begin to find earth's bitterness sweet and its hard lessons easy. The secret is acceptance—saying yes to God as he permits those events that bring about our humbling. It is his will that we are in this hard place; in that will we must rest. We must accept what he has permitted and let it work in us what he has willed.

George MacDonald wrote of his own dishonor, "I learned that it is better . . . for a proud man to fall and be humbled than to hold up his head in pride and fancied innocence. I learned that he that will be a hero will barely be a man. He who has been humbled is sure of his manhood."

THE BEAUTY
OF HOLINESS

He hath a daily beauty . . . that makes me ugly.

—William Shakespeare

There's a remarkable story about David in the closing chapters of 2 Samuel that tells me more about "the man after God's own heart" than any other description:

During harvest time, three of the thirty chief men came down to David at the cave of Adullam, while a band of Philistines was encamped in the Valley of Rephaim. At that time David was in the stronghold, and the Philistine garrison was at Bethlehem. David longed for water and said, "Oh, that someone would get me a drink of water from the well near the gate of Bethlehem!" So the three mighty men broke through the Philistine lines, drew water from the well near the gate of Bethlehem and carried it back to David. But he refused to drink it; instead, he poured it out before the LORD. "Far be it from me, O LORD, to do this!" he

said. "Is it not the blood of men who went at the risk
of their lives?" And David would not drink it"
(23:13–17).

All we know about this event is what we read here. It's
placed in the text as one example of the love and loyalty of
David's tough little army and the quality of David's life that
drew good men around him.

The event occurred during the last stages of David's
conflict with the Philistines, his mortal enemy. The main
Philistine force had moved into the mountains and taken up a
position near the city of Jerusalem. Their aim was to defend
the city, which was then in Canaanite hands and was probably
a Philistine dependency. In so doing they cut off David from
the northern tribes from which he drew much of his support.
His situation seemed hopeless.

In a moment of homesickness and deep yearning for a
former, less complicated time, David uttered a quiet wish for
a drink from a well near Bethlehem he recalled from his
youth. It was just a wish, nothing more, but three of his men
heard him and took him at his word.

These three men were probably the three whose exploits are
supplied in the preceding context who had distinguished
themselves in holy war with the Philistines (23:8–12).

There was Josheb-Basshebeth, who "raised his spear
against eight hundred men, whom he killed in one encounter"
(23:8).

There was Eleazar who "was with David when they
taunted the Philistines gathered at Pas Dammim for battle.
Then the men of Israel retreated, but he stood his ground and
struck down the Philistines till his hand grew tired and froze
to the sword (23:9–10).

And finally there was Shammah who "took his stand in
the middle of a field. He defended it and struck the Philistines
down" (23:11–12).

It's enough to say these were three tough dudes!

Without a word these men crept out of the stronghold at Adullum, fought their way through the Philistine lines to the well on the northeast side of the city of Bethlehem, drew water, fought their way back to David and presented him with their gift.

David looked at the blood and bruises on their bodies and poured out the water as an offering to the Lord. It had cost too much; it was too precious to drink.

Alexander the Great did the same thing on his march to Persia. At one point, when offered a helmet full of water by a traveler, he poured it out because none of his weary, wind-parched men had water to drink.

Perhaps he had read the story of David. He may have been familiar with certain portions of the Bible. Tradition suggests that on Alexander's march through Judah, one of Israel's priests handed him a portion of Daniel's prophecy to read. Perhaps he gave him more than we know.

In any case, these stories speak to some intuition we have of what a good man ought to be. They describe the state of a real man's soul.

When reading about David and his mighty men with a couple of my friends one day, we fell into thinking about this extraordinary act. After some reflective discussion, one of the men in the group leaned back in his chair and muttered to himself, "What a beautiful guy."

"Beautiful" sounded odd to me at the time, especially when applied to a rugged old warrior like David, but it's exactly the right word. The Bible itself speaks of "the beauty of holiness" (Psalm 29:2; 96:9) as though true goodness is something beautiful to see. It is. Peter puts it this way:

> Live such good lives among the pagans that, though
> they accuse you of doing wrong, they may see your

good deeds and glorify God on the day he visits us
(1 Peter 2:12).

The word twice translated "good" in this text means
"beautiful." In that sense David was indeed a "beautiful guy."

Nice guys and good old boys

The best way to see the true beauty of manhood is to see
it in Jesus. Those who knew him best said that he was a good
man, "full of grace and truth." Everything he did was truthful,
and yet he was unfailingly gracious.

There is "truth" that isn't gracious at all. It may be the
antithesis of falsehood, but it's also the antithesis of beauty. It
was grace linked with truth that made Jesus the man that he
was.

I think of that occasion on which his disciples were
arguing about who was the greatest. Who could have blamed
our Lord if he had blasted them? But he did not. He rather
girded himself with a towel, and began to wash their feet. He
who was the greatest of all became the servant of all. Don't
you think his disciples thought, "What a beautiful man"?

And then there was that leper Jesus encountered when he
was teaching in one of the little villages of Galilee. Luke says
the man was "full of leprosy"—a medical expression for an
advanced case of the disease. He was all lesions, running
sores, and grotesque stumps, discolored and disfigured,
shocking in his ugliness, a gross caricature of what a man was
intended to be.

Jesus, "moved with compassion," reached out and *hugged*
him. He didn't have to touch him. He could have cured the
man with a word from afar. Yet there was every need in the
world to hug this ugly, awful man because no one else had
done so. Don't you think that man went away thinking, "What
a beautiful man"?

There was that day Jesus was teaching in the temple, when he was interrupted by shouts and sounds of scuffling and a group of clergymen barged in and unceremoniously dumped a woman, rumpled, disheveled, and defiant at this feet. "Teacher, this woman was caught in the act of adultery," they said triumphantly. "In the Law, Moses commanded us to stone such women. Now what do you say?" (John 8:4–5).

"Daughter," he said, looking at the woman with his kind eyes, "I don't condemn you. Go and sin no more." Don't you think she went away thinking, "What a beautiful man"?

I think of the dirty little street urchins of that day who used to tag along behind Jesus and climb into his lap, and I remember the adage that a truly good man is one "around whose gate and garden children are unafraid to play." His disciples wanted to shoo them away. Jesus gathered them into his arms and blessed them. Don't you think they remembered him as a beautiful man?

These vignettes reflect a manly beauty that's hard to put into words. It's more than being decent, ethical, and right. It has a rugged, "more than" quality about it that Jesus summed up with the question, "What are you doing *more than* others?" (Matthew 5:47). It's a matter of doing things *beautifully*.

True goodness is not doing extraordinary things. It is doing ordinary things in an extraordinary way. Pascal said, "The strength of a man's virtue must not be measured by his efforts but by his ordinary life." It is not so much a matter of overt religious behavior as it is a gracious, winsome spirit with which we do everything.

Jesus was inclined to be very stern with those who wore their religion on their sleeves: "Be careful not to do your 'acts of righteousness' before men, to be seen by them," he warned. "If you do, you will have no reward from your Father in heaven (Matthew 6:1). We'll never hear God's "Atta boy!" that way.

Authentic goodness is something more subtle. Howard Butt described it this way: "It is not a way of doing special things. It is a special way of doing everything. Can I talk to a woman as Jesus did? Or ask for a drink of water; or cook fish; or walk through my hometown; or talk to my men? It is basins and towels and washing feet. I'm not supposed to be a gilt-edged spook with wings making a holy hum. I'm supposed to be a normal, natural, down to earth human being, full of creation's practical Spirit."

It's *how* we play the game: *how* we conduct ourselves when we play a round of golf; *how* we behave ourselves at a business conference; *how* we talk to our wives and our children; *how* we respond to slights and injustices. It is doing *everything* we do with a certain elegance and style.

Rudyard Kipling has captured something of this idea in his poem "If":

> *If you can keep your head when all about you*
> *Are losing theirs and blaming it on you,*
> *If you can trust yourself when all men doubt you,*
> *But make allowance for their doubting too;*
> *If you can wait and not be tired by waiting,*
> *Or being lied about, don't deal in lies,*
> *Or being hated, don't give way to hating,*
> *And yet don't look too good, nor talk too wise:*
>
> . . .
>
> *If you can talk with crowds and keep your virtue,*
> *Or walk with Kings—nor lose the common touch,*
> *If neither foes nor loving friends can hurt you,*
> *If all men count with you, but none too much:*
> *If you can fill the unforgiving minute*
> *With sixty seconds' worth of distance run,*
> *Yours is the Earth and everything that's in it,*
> *And—which is more—you'll be a Man, my son!*

I'm reminded of a friend of mine, Brian Morgan, who came to Stanford University in the seventies with hopes of becoming an Olympic gymnast. As a young man someone had planted Paul's word in his mind, "Glorify God in your body" (1 Corinthians 6:20).

His plan was to hone his body to perfection and then, having achieved a certain measure of athletic prominence, give God all the credit for his success. But Brian was an athlete who matured early and got no better. In fact, he got worse. His senior year was a disaster.

The coup de grâce came at an NCAA meet when he fell off the high bar and landed on his head. It was hard on his head, but good for his soul, he said. That's when it came to him that what Paul actually said was, glorify God *in* your body, not *with* it. It was far more important for him to be gracious in dishonor than to win big and look good. It's that subtle shift in thought that represents the beauty of holiness.

What hath God wrought?

We cannot, by moral effort, change ourselves one iota. Everything that needs to be done in our souls can only be done by God. "All virtue is a miracle," said Augustine.

Change creeps to us. It is the fruit of our association with Jesus. As we draw close to him day by day—walking with him, talking to him, listening to his words, relying on him, asking for his help—his character begins to rub off on us. Quietly and unobtrusively his influence softens our wills, making us thirsty for his righteousness. In his quiet love he takes all that's unworthy in us and gradually turns it into something beautiful.

Howard Butt writes, "The dusty, pedestrian duties of life demand God Almighty in us. It takes as much of the power of God for me to go to my office and sit at the desk and talk on the phone (as I should), to go through my regular routine, as it does for others to preach a sermon, or write a religious book."

There may be sins within your heart that have long resisted control. Do what you may they still defy you. But if you hand over the conflict to God he will subdue those sins in his own time and in his own way. What you cannot do, he can. Whenever the old temptation arises, as soon as you are aware of it, lift your heart to Jesus and reckon on him to cope with it. He will fight for you if you will stand fast and wait.

God is at work in you. Call it mysticism or whatever—the name matters little. What matters is that the God of the universe has promised to live in you and reproduce his life in you. "Without him you can do nothing"; with him anything is possible. "To have Christ within is to realize your creed not as something you have to bear, but something by which you are *borne*, this is true Christianity" (James Stewart). This is the only goodness that can be called truly good.

Gentle persuasion

Few things are harder to put up with than a good example.

—Mark Twain

God's work is always good. It imparts an unforgettable beauty and fragrance to our lives that sticks in people's minds. There is a catchy little psalm that enshrines that truth, one verse of which reads, "The upright man shines in the darkness like a light: he is gracious, compassionate and righteous." That person, the poet goes on to say, "will be remembered *forever*" (Psalm 112:4, 6).

Men who put themselves in God's hand to be shaped and used have a profound effect upon others. Herman Melville in his story *Billy Budd* tells of the reaction of Billy's captain when the young sailor was conscripted from his boat for His Majesty's service. He objected strenuously to seaman Budd's leaving because of the impact he had on the crew: "My forecastle was a rat-pit of quarrels," he said. "But Billy came; and it was like a Catholic priest striking peace in an Irish shindy [fight]. Not that he preached to them or said or did anything in particular; but a virtue went out of him, sugaring the sour ones."

Those whom God is making good have an extraordinary effect on others. Paul writes, "For we are to God the aroma of Christ among those who are being saved and those who are perishing. To the one we are the smell of death; to the other, the fragrance of life" (2 Corinthians 2:15–16).

Godliness can repel. In Billy Budd's case it led to his death. Paul points out that to some we smell like something dead. But to others we leave behind the sweet fragrance of Christ, a subtle ambience that lingers and leaves others longing for more (2 Corinthians 2:14–15).

Some years ago my wife, Carolyn, and I attended a concert in Boise that featured an alto soloist who awed us with her rich voice and astonishing range. On the way out, a young woman who had accompanied us, herself a musician, said to Carolyn, "I wish I could take lessons from her." Would that we so lived that others would want to take lessons from us.

I think of Peter's words again: "Live such good lives among the pagans that . . . they may see your good deeds and glorify God on the day he visits us" (1 Peter 2:12), or, as one translation renders it, "My friends, do you want to win your unbelieving friends? Then whatever you do, do it beautifully."

George MacDonald has written, "If you try too hard to make people good you will only make them worse. The only way to make people good is to *be* good—remember the beam and the mote. The time for speaking comes rarely, the time for *being* never departs."

To be or not to be

To be or not to be? That is the question.

—William Shakespeare

Hamlet's question is probably the best known line in English literature. It had to do with the question of whether it was better for him to *be* ("to suffer the slings and arrows of outrageous fortune"), or to *do* ("to take up arms against a sea of troubles and by opposing end them"). His question is our question as well.

There is a time and place for both, but God puts a premium on *being*. Being always comes before doing, though we're inclined to go about our business the other way 'round.

Peter, in his second epistle, urges us to "make every effort to add to [our] faith goodness; and to goodness, knowledge; and to knowledge, self-control; and to self-control, perseverance; and to perseverance, godliness; and to godliness, brotherly kindness; and to brotherly kindness, love. For," Peter concludes, "if [we] possess these qualities in increasing measure, they will keep [us] from being ineffective and unproductive" (1:5–8).

Effectiveness and productivity stem from what we are. Though we may seem to be doing nothing worthwhile, we are doing everything worthwhile if our lives are styled by God's grace.

Set aside through sickness or seclusion we can still be fruitful. Bed-ridden or house-bound, we can be productive. We don't have to be good for anything to be useful; just good. What matters is what we are.

Will Campbell, an eccentric Yale-trained hillbilly gospel preacher who ministers in the backwoods of Tennessee, comes straight to the point:

> Somebody is always winding up my [preaching] sessions by charging, "What you're saying, it seems, is just, 'Do nothing.' And when I hear that, that's when I know I'm beginning to come through. That's when I say, "Brother, just nail that one down—now you got the message. Do nothing. Instead, *be* something. Before you start trying to figure out what you should do about all the world's woes, just be what you are—a follower of Christ. When that happens, then you won't have to ask what to do—you'll already know."

Campbell is right: "Be something!" Doing comes naturally if we're becoming what God has created us to be.

There comes a time

There comes a time when you better stop trying to figure out who you are and start living like the man you want to be.

—Bruce Springsteen

Springsteen is right. It's time to live like the men we want to be—not the puny, effete figment-men offered up by our culture, but authentic men who in the mess and muddle of the marketplace, in the midst of its misunderstandings and misjudgments will make visible the beauty of the invisible God.

If you want it you can have it, but God must do it. The only way to learn manliness is to put yourself in God's hands and ask him to change you into the man you long to be. "Faithful is he who has called you and *he* will do it" (1 Thessalonians 5:24).

Do you recognize the deformity and ugliness of your character? Ask God to change it to be like his. Do you seek the beauty of holiness? "He will be a diadem of beauty," as one of Israel's poets said.

Does evil predominate? Are you troubled by your anger, touchiness, defensiveness, irritability, and closet perversions? He is at hand, slowly but inexorably molding you into the man you want to be. Press on. You can do all things through the one who strengthens you.

Tolstoy tells a story about an old cobbler, Martin Avdyeeich, who lost his wife and his little child, Kapitoshka, and then his faith. One day an aged peasant-pilgrim came from a nearby monastery and began to talk to him about his despair.

"What then is a man to live for?" asked Avdyeeich. The old man answered: "For God, Martin! He gave thee life, and for Him therefore must thou live. When thou dost begin to live for Him, thou wilt grieve about nothing more, and all things will come easy to thee."

Martin then asked: "And how must one live for God?" "Christ hath shown us the way," the pilgrim answered. "Thou knowest thy letters. Buy the Gospels and read; there thou wilt find out how to live for God. There everything is explained."

Tolstoy goes on with his story: "These words made the heart of Avdyeeich burn within him, and he went the same day and bought for himself a New Testament printed in very large type, and began to read . . . . And the more he read, the more clearly he understood what God wanted of him, and how it behooved him to live for God; and his heart grew lighter and lighter continually . . . .

"It happened once that Martin was up reading till very late. He was reading St. Luke's Gospel. He was reading the sixth chapter, and as he read he came to the words: 'And to him that smiteth thee on the one cheek, offer also the other.' Avdyeeich read these words through and through. He took off his glasses, laid them on the book, rested his elbow on the table, and fell a-thinking. And he began to measure his own life by these words. And he thought to himself, 'O Lord, help me!' "

We cannot adorn ourselves. "In vain you make yourself beautiful," Jeremiah insists (4:30). No, with David, we can only "gaze upon the beauty of the Lord" (Psalm 27:4) and ask him to transform us into his image, from one degree of likeness to the next.

"O Lord, help me!" This is our prayer as well.

Let the beauty of Jesus be seen in me—
All his wonderful passion and purity!
O Thou Spirit divine, all my nature refine,
Til the beauty of Jesus be seen in me.

—Tom Jones

DEAR ABBY

There is a certain kind of meekness—of submission— that brings out the worst in a man, whereas that same man, faced by spirit and determination might be a different creature.

—Agatha Christie

Isabella Thoburn, a nineteenth-century missionary to India wrote, "No man ever rises higher than the point to which he elevates women." There's a wealth of wisdom in those words.

Here's a story about David that illustrates well her proverb. It begins with Samuel's death. Samuel was David's last chance for reconciliation with Saul. With Samuel's death David's chances with Saul vanished, and David withdrew into the wilderness of Paran—a vast semi-arid region that stretched between Judah and the Sinai.

In that place David was relatively free from Saul's insane pursuit and could be of service to his countrymen by protecting their flocks from attacks of marauding desert tribes. There one day, David and his men came across the man the Bible calls The Big Fool:

> A certain man in Maon, who had property there at Carmel, was very wealthy. He had a thousand goats and three thousand sheep, which he was shearing in Carmel. His name was Nabal and his wife's name was Abigail. She was an intelligent and beautiful woman, but her husband, a Calebite, was surly and mean in his dealings" (1 Samuel 25:2–3).

Nabal was mismatched with his wife, Abigail. She's described as a beautiful woman—beautiful of form and face—but her beauty was more than skin deep; she was "intelligent," a word that means insightful and perceptive.

Nabal, on the other hand, was a churlish, intractable man, "surly and mean in his dealings." The word translated *surly* means "hard, cruel, severe." This must have been a very unhappy marriage.

What kind of fool am I?

Nabal's name means "fool"—an ominous designation. It's unlikely that a parent would saddle a kid with a name like that. I rather think "Nabal" was a tongue-in-cheek corruption of the man's real name, but in whatever way he got the handle, he deserved it. As Abigail herself said, in our modern slang, "Fool is his name and fool is his game" (25:25).

The Hebrew language knows five kinds of fools. In ascending order of foolishness, there is the *petî,* from a Hebrew root that means "to be open." The *petî* is naive and untutored, a "simpleton." This is the way we come into the world; this is the natural-born fool. This is the young man who watches *Beavis and Butthead* and thinks he knows everything there is to know about life. If he doesn't receive serious instruction, he will soon graduate into serious folly.

Then there is the *kesîl*, from a root that means "to be dull, obtuse." The *kesîl* is a little to the dark side of the *petî*. He is insensitive to wisdom and disinterested in learning about it.

The third fool is the *'ewîl*. The root suggests that this fool is characterized by stubbornness. He is entrenched in his resistance to truth—headstrong, willful, unteachable. "Don't confuse me with the facts," he says. "My mind is made up."

The *lîtz* is darker still. The root indicates that he is full of scorn. He is the "scoffer" of King James fame. This is the cynical, sneering university professor or student who sits above God's wisdom and mocks those who take it seriously.

And finally there is the *nabal*, a composite of all other fools, and the worst of the lot—the fool to end all fools. This is the person who follows his own rules and acts as if there is no God. "The fool [*nabal*] says in his heart, 'There is no God.' They are corrupt, and their ways are vile" (Psalm 53:1). Abigail's Nabal was the ultimate fool.

Isaiah describes the final fool this way: "The fool [*nabal*] speaks folly, his mind is busy with evil: He practices ungodliness and spreads error concerning the LORD; the hungry he leaves empty and from the thirsty he withholds water" (Isaiah 32:6).

Socrates divided the world into two types of people: the wise who know they are fools and the fools who think they are wise. It's wise to know what kind of fools we are.

The "dog"

One more thing. Nabal is also called a "Calebite," which could mean nothing more than that he was a descendent of Caleb, the old, Israelite warrior who settled Mt. Hebron. But *caleb* also means "dog."

In those days dogs were not pets. They were mean-spirited, snarling scavengers, more like jackals than the dogs we know. If the author intends us to understand the term this way, it's a reference to Nabal's cynical, sneering contempt of others. (Our word *cynic* comes from *cynicus*, the Latin word for dog and, meaning doglike and churlish.)

The festival

Nabal's residence was in the city of Maon, but his "business" was at Carmel, a place about half an hour northwest, where he kept his vast herds. The time mentioned in 1 Samuel was a special occasion: sheep-shearing time.

Sheep-shearing was traditionally a festive event, much like our old-time harvest festivals, when hearts were open and hospitality was extended. People gathered from far and wide to share the joy of the occasion.

It was in the spirit of such an occurrence that David sent ten of his men to Carmel with this message:

"Go up to Nabal at Carmel and greet him in my name. Say to him: 'Long life to you! Good health to you and your household! And good health to all that is yours!

" 'Now I hear that it is sheep-shearing time. When your shepherds were with us, we did not ill-treat them, and the whole time they were at Carmel nothing of theirs was missing. Ask your own servants and they will tell you. Therefore be favorable toward my young men, since we come at a festive time. Please give your servants and your son David whatever you can find for them' " (25:5–8).

It was only right for David to make this request. David and his men needed food and drink, and festivals were times when the impoverished were gathered in. Furthermore, David and his men had watched over Nabal's herds and herdsmen and, as Nabal's servants put it, he had not suffered the slightest loss (25:15–16). Nabal owed David this favor.

David's men gave Nabal his message. Then they waited—
and waited, and waited. (One method of intimidating others and
empowering oneself is deliberately to keep others waiting!)

Finally, Nabal answered David's men,

> "Who is this David? Who is this son of Jesse? Many
> servants are breaking away from their masters these
> days. Why should I take my bread and water, and the
> meat I have slaughtered for my shearers, and give it to
> men coming from who knows where?"
>
> David's men returned and reported every word
> (25:10–12).

David's request was denied in the most insulting,
contemptuous way. Nabal knew who David was and what he
stood for, but cared nothing for David and God's plan to bring
salvation to the earth through his anointed servant.

When the affront was reported to David he reacted with
predictable passion:

> David said to his men, "Put on your swords!" So they put
> on their swords, and David put on his. About four
> hundred men went up with David, while two hundred
> stayed with the supplies (25:13).

Testosterone took over! "Strap on your guns," David
shouted to his companions. "Let's take this oaf out!" And he
and his angry young men set off to chasten the old fool. But
David was the fool on this occasion—his passion was brutal
and cold.

Injustice takes us by surprise and arouses us to anger. We
may not be driven to kill like David, but we still feel like
murdering someone. Our passion, like David's becomes bitter
and murderous. It's not justice that impells us, but personal
pique.

Abigail to the rescue

David was playing the fool on this occasion, but God stepped in and averted the massacre. He moved one of Nabal's men to alert Abigail:

> "David sent messengers from the desert to give our master his greetings, but he hurled insults at them. Yet these men were very good to us. They did not ill-treat us, and the whole time we were out in the fields near them nothing was missing. Night and day they were a wall around us all the time we were herding our sheep near them. Now think it over and see what you can do, because disaster is hanging over our master and his whole household. He is such a wicked man that no one can talk to him" (25:14–17).

Abigail lost no time. She immediately set out to intercept David.

> She took two hundred loaves of bread, two skins of wine, five dressed sheep, five seahs of roasted grain, a hundred cakes of raisins and two hundred cakes of pressed figs, and loaded them on donkeys. She told her servants, "Go on ahead; I'll follow you." But she did not tell her husband Nabal.
> As she came riding her donkey into a mountain ravine, there were David and his men descending toward her, and she met them (25:18–20).

The Hebrew for "mountain ravine" is literally "the "covert" or "hidden place" of the mountain—some topographical feature that hid Abigail and David from one another's view until the last minute.

David was fuming—ranting and raving, muttering under his breath:

"It's been useless—all my watching over this fellow's property in the desert so that nothing of his was missing. He has paid me back evil for good. May God deal with David, be it ever so severely, if by morning I leave alive one male of all who belong to him!" (25:21–22).

At that very moment, Abigail rounded the corner and found herself face to face with David. She fell on her face at the feet of the young, would-be king and uttered some of the purest words ever spoken.

"Please let your servant speak to you; hear what your servant has to say. May my lord pay no attention to that wicked Nabal. He is just like his name—his name is Fool, and folly goes with him. But as for me, your servant, I did not see the men my master sent.

"Now since the LORD has kept you, my master, from bloodshed and from avenging yourself with your own hands, as surely as the LORD lives and as you live, may your enemies and all who intend to harm my master be like Nabal. And let this gift, which your servant has brought to my master, be given to the men who follow you. Please forgive your servant's offense, for the LORD will certainly make a lasting dynasty for my master, because he fights the LORD's battles. Let no wrongdoing be found in you as long as you live. Even though someone is pursuing you to take your life, the life of my master will be bound securely in the bundle of the living by the LORD your God. But the lives of your enemies he will hurl away as from the pocket of a sling. When the LORD has done for my master every good thing he promised concerning him and has appointed him leader over Israel, my master will not have on his conscience the staggering burden of needless bloodshed or of having avenged himself. And when the LORD has brought my master success, remember your servant" (25:24–31).

Abby's advice

"Unsolicited advice is criticism," someone has said. At least that's how we perceive it. But there are some things to note about Abigail's advice that helped to make the medicine go down.

She demonstrates a remarkable degree of sensitivity, asking David's tolerance, acknowledging that it will not be easy for him to hear her counsel.

She understood human resistance to advice and asked David's forbearance. (She had learned how to handle an angry man. She had lived with one for years.)

There's a certain amount of exaggerated, overstated Eastern courtesy going on here, but two traits come through —meekness and tranquility. Abigail doesn't engage in an emotional tirade. She is remarkably composed given her situation. She demonstrates what Peter calls "a gentle and quiet spirit, which is of great worth in God's sight" (1 Peter 3:4). (It should be pointed out that meekness and tranquility are not attributes enjoined on women alone. These are not feminine or masculine traits but godly traits [see Matthew 5:5; 2 Thessalonians 3:12].)

Advice and counsel should always be offered in this spirit. "A *gentle* answer turns away wrath," the wise man says. Paul agrees: "Brothers, if someone is caught in a sin, you who are spiritual should restore him *gently*" (Galatians 6:1).

Her message

The first piece of advice Abigail gave David is to let fools be fools. Nabal was a "Son of Belial"—a godless man. Leave him alone in his insanity, she says.

Wise words! The proverbs tell us, "Do not speak to a fool, for he will scorn the wisdom of your words" (Proverbs 23:9). "Do not answer a fool according to his folly, or you will be like him yourself" (Proverbs 26:4).

Chronically arrogant people are impossible to reason with. Appeal to them once or twice, bring other witnesses to bear, but in the end, if a man or woman will not listen to wisdom, we must leave them alone. "Though you grind a fool in a mortar," says the wise man, "grinding him like grain with a pestle, you will not remove his folly from him" (Proverbs 27:22). The only way to handle people who are not teachable and not convinced of the value of humility and modesty is to leave them alone.

Social scientists working in the realm of learning theory talk about a phenomenon they call an "extinction-burst." Some people must do their insane thing, they say, until they self-destruct. There's no other way to bring them to their senses. (The story of the Prodigal may be an example of the truth of this theory.)

Jesus' disciples came to him once and remarked on the tomfoolery of the Pharisees. He replied, "Every plant that my heavenly Father has not planted will be pulled up by the roots; *leave them [alone]*" (Matthew 15:13–14).

I recently came across a story that seems apropos. A terrifying lion encountered a cowardly monkey on a jungle train and pinned him to the ground. "Who's the king of the beasts!" the lion roared in his face. "Y-y-you are!" the monkey stammered. The lion let him go.

Next the lion came across an elephant. He roared out insults to the elephant and asked him the same question. With his trunk the elephant reached out, picked him up, and slammed him against a tree fifty feet away. "Well," said the lion meekly, as he dusted himself off and slunk away, "just because you don't know the answer, you don't have to get rough about it."

The moral is clear: Leave a fool alone and let life rough him up. Maybe he'll get the lesson, maybe not. In either case it's not our job to chasten fools.

The second piece of advice Abigail gave was to let God deal with fools. "Learning is remembering," said Plato. Nothing Abigail told David was news. He was aware of these truths, had written about them, and practiced them in the forbearance he showed Saul. Abigail simply reminded David of truths his fury had caused him to forget.

The main thing was that he must trust God and not take matters into his own hands. God had been faithful to keep David from shedding blood in the past, and he would deal with David's enemies in the future. God was the one who chastened fools.

Abigail knew the word: "Do not seek revenge . . ." (Leviticus 19:18). "It is mine to avenge; I will repay. In due time their foot will slip; their day of disaster is near and their doom rushes upon them" (Deuteronomy 32:35).

God treads the winepress of his wrath *alone*. Leave the avenging to God, she pleads. God will make all your enemies as Nabal—showing them to be fools, with the ruin and self-destruction that the name implies. David must not defend himself nor work for his own deliverance. He was engaged in the "*LORD's* battles," not his own. David must wait for God to work out his judgment in his own way and in his time.

The alternative was to rob God of his honor and rob himself of a pure conscience. Abigail knew that one day David would ascend to the throne and when he did so it was her prayer that he would know that he had not sought the throne by ungodly means—means that would leave him with profound regret.

Walter Brueggerman writes, "All [Abigail's] actions are informed by her conviction that David has a 'sure house' (vs. 28). That house is made sure by the restraint of David and the decisive work of the Lord."

God had given David authority to bring salvation and deliverance to others (see 1 Samuel 23:4), but, as Abigail reminded him, he must not use his hand for his own salvation. This the Lord must do. Thus in the gospels Jesus saves, heals, and delivers others, but he will not use his power to save himself. This God must do.

Paul applies this principle to all believers: "Do not repay anyone evil for evil. Be careful to do what is right in the eyes of everybody. If it is possible, as far as it depends on you, live at peace with everyone. Do not take revenge, my friends, but leave room for God's wrath, for it is written: 'It is mine to avenge; I will repay,' says the Lord. On the contrary: 'If your enemy is hungry, feed him; if he is thirsty, give him something to drink. In doing this, you will heap burning coals on his head.' Do not be overcome by evil, but overcome evil with good" (Romans 12:17–21).

David's enlightenment

David, duly humbled, came to his senses:

David said to Abigail, "Praise be to the LORD, the God of Israel, who has sent you today to meet me. May you be blessed for your good judgment and for keeping me from bloodshed this day and from avenging myself with my own hands. Otherwise, as surely as the LORD, the God of Israel, lives, who has kept me from harming you, if you had not come quickly to meet me, not one male belonging to Nabal would have been left alive by daybreak."

Then David accepted from her hand what she had brought to him and said, "Go home in peace. I have heard your words and granted your request" (1 Samuel 25:32–35).

Proverbs says the earth shakes a "fool who is full of food" (Proverbs 30:22). Here's a case study:

> When Abigail went to Nabal, he was in the house
> holding a banquet like that of a king. He was in high
> spirits and very drunk. So she told him nothing until
> daybreak. Then in the morning, when Nabal was
> sober, his wife told him all these things, and his heart
> failed him and he became like a stone. About ten days
> later, the LORD struck Nabal and he died (1 Samuel
> 25:36–38).

When Abigail reported what she had done Nabal was so
enraged that he had a stroke and sank into a coma. Ten days
later he died. "The LORD struck Nabal and he died," the text
declares. Rarely does God's justice come so swiftly. His mills
normally grind more slowly. But they do grind exceedingly
small. "Though with patience he stands waiting; with
exactness grinds he *all*."

> When David heard that Nabal was dead, he said,
> "Praise be to the LORD, who has upheld my cause
> against Nabal for treating me with contempt. He has
> kept his servant from doing wrong and has brought
> Nabal's wrongdoing down on his own head."
>   Then David sent word to Abigail, asking her to
> become his wife. His servants went to Carmel and said
> to Abigail, "David has sent us to you to take you to
> become his wife."
>   She bowed down with her face to the ground and
> said, "Here is your maidservant, ready to serve you and
> wash the feet of my master's servants." Abigail quickly
> got on a donkey and, attended by her five maids, went
> with David's messengers and became his wife
> (1 Samuel 25:39–42).

That's an interesting assessment on the part of David! "*He*
has kept his servant from doing wrong . . . ." David heard
God's voice in Abigail's wise counsel.

Abigail became David's wife-in-exile, though she soon after passed off the scene and it's assumed that she died shortly after David became king at Hebron. She did not enjoy the fruit of his reign, but her influence lingered on. Abigail and David had one son whom David named *Chileab* —"A Father's Restraint" (2 Samuel 3:3). His name comes from the verb translated "kept [his servant]" in the text cited above, surely to recall the role that Abigail played in curbing David's rash and impulsive soul and keeping him from evil. Abigail had marked her man forever.

There are two kinds of men in the world: those who listen to wise women, and those who don't. Men who treat women with disdain and fail to take them seriously simply because they are women have missed what the Bible has been saying all along: For those who love God, "there is neither male nor female" (Galatians 3:27). When it comes to wisdom, gender makes no difference at all.

David took women as he found them, unlike some men who have their uncertain male dignity to defend. "The way of a fool seems right to him, but a wise man listens to advice" (Proverbs 12:15).

David listened to wisdom and grew strong. Unlike Nabal, and some other men I know, David was no fool.

As for us men we must learn from women as well as men, never disregarding or minimizing a contribution simply because it's offered by a woman. That's sexism, and it's sin. It's significant to me that wisdom is personified as a woman in Proverbs. Perhaps they have a special gift for it.

We must not disparage the women in our lives or denigrate their achievements. We must show them honor as joint heirs of eternal life (1 Peter 3:7). As George MacDonald says, "*Woman* ought to be the dearest word to every man, next to God."

THE HARDER
THEY FALL

Alas! how easily things go wrong!
A sigh too deep or a kiss too long,
And then comes a mist and a weeping rain,
And life is never the same again.

—George MacDonald

I keep seeing my friends fall. I wonder why they do it? What causes a man to trash his marriage and all he's worked for, for a transient affair?

Take David, for example—Israel's greatest king, the "man after God's own heart." He fell for Uriah's pretty, young wife, Bathsheba.

It happened "in the spring, at the time when kings go off to war" (2 Samuel 11:1). That spring, however, in fatal lethargy, David's fancy turned to thoughts of love. "One evening David got up from his bed and walked around on the roof of his palace" (11:2).

From there, he had a commanding view of Jerusalem and could look down into neighboring courtyards. As he surveyed his city, his eyes fell upon a young woman taking a bath. The text says she was *very* beautiful (11:2).

If the woman seems immodest, you must remember there was no indoor plumbing in those days. Baths were normally taken outdoors in enclosed courtyards.

David was entranced! He sent someone "to find out about her" (1:3), whereupon, one of his friends tried to end the affair: "Isn't this Bathsheba, the daughter of Eliam, and the wife of Uriah the Hittite?" (11:3) he asked. She was a married woman—married in fact to one of David's close friends, an old army buddy, Uriah.

David, however, would not be denied. He "sent messengers to get her." One wrong thing led to another, "and he slept with her. . . . Then she went back home." Later, we're told, "she sent word to David, saying, 'I am pregnant!' " (11:4–5).

David knew he was in big trouble! Bathsheba's husband was engaged in the siege of the Ammonite city of Rabbah and would be away for several months. Anyone could count to nine. In other lands kings were the law, but not in Israel. No one was above God's Word. And adultery was serious sin.

But David, always a man of action, devised a plan to avert the consequences of his affair. He sent word to Joab to release Uriah from his command and send him to Jerusalem, ostensibly to report on the war, but in reality to bring him home to Bathsheba. When the old warrior arrived, David perfunctorily listened to his briefing and then dismissed Uriah to his home: "Go down to your house and wash your feet," he said with a twinkle in his eye.

But Uriah "slept at the entrance of the palace with all his master's servant and did not go down to his house" (11:9). The old soldier explained, "The ark and Israel and Judah are staying in tents, and my master Joab and my lord's men are camping in the open fields. How could I go to my house to eat and drink and to lie with my wife? As surely as you live, I will not do such a thing."

David replied, " 'Stay here one more day, and tomorrow I will let you go.' So Uriah remained in Jerusalem that day and the next. At David's invitation, he ate and drank with him, and David made him drunk. But in the evening Uriah went out to sleep on his mat among his master's servants; he did not go home" (11:10–13).

Uriah may have heard palace rumors of Bathsheba's dalliance or he may just have felt his integrity as a professional soldier was at stake. He would not go home while those under his command were separated from their wives and families. Despite David's repeated efforts to persuade Uriah, the stern old Hittite refused. Even the expedient of getting him drunk failed. Each evening Uriah rolled out his sleeping bag on the floor of the palace guardroom and slept with the rest of the troops.

Time was running out. In desperation David put a contract on his good friend's life, ordering General Joab to "place Uriah in the front line where fighting is fiercest. Then withdraw from him, so that he will be struck down and die" (11:15).

Joab, who was no fool, refused to follow David's directive. The plan was so obviously treacherous that he altered it: "While Joab had the city under siege, he put Uriah at a place where he knew the strongest defenders were. When the men of the city came out and fought against Joab, some of the men in David's army fell; moreover, Uriah the Hittite was dead" (11:16–17).

Joab placed Uriah where his intelligence reports told him the fighting would be most intense, in the hope that Uriah would be slain. Joab's plan, though less obviously treacherous than David's, resulted in greater loss of life. There were many Israeli widows and orphans who wept that day.

Joab then sent a runner to David with a report on the battle. He knew David would be critical of his tactics and the resultant loss of life, but, he hastened to report that Uriah had been killed (11:18–22). "Ah," mused David, "the sword devours one as well as the other" (11:25). The fortunes of war. *C'est la vie.*

When Bathsheba heard that her husband was dead, she mourned for him, and when her brief period of mourning was over, David "had her brought to his house, and she became his wife and bore him a son" (11:26–27).

David moved with inappropriate haste, but marriage put a legal and final end to the sordid affair, or so David thought. God knew, and "the thing David had done displeased the LORD" (11:27).

A year passed, during which time David deteriorated physically and emotionally. As he later described his feelings:

> When I kept silent,
> > my bones wasted away
> > through my groaning all day long.
> For day and night
> > your hand was heavy upon me;
> my strength was sapped
> > as in the heat of summer (Psalm 32:3–4).

His gnawing conscience kept him restless and melancholy. Every waking moment was filled with misery; at night he tossed and turned. Anxiety sapped his energy. His depression deepened with every passing day.

Second Samuel 12:26–31 describes a telling event during the year that David tried to evade his conscience. (The account is displaced chronologically, actually occurring shortly after Bathsheba and David were married.) Joab captured the citadel guarding the water supply of the Ammonite city of Rabbah and knew that the fall of the fortress was imminent. He called for David to lead the army in the final assault. When the city fell, David massacred the population of Rabbah and her sister villages and "sawed them with saws and with iron picks and with axes."

We cannot mitigate David's sin. Judah's most illustrious ruler, sweet singer of Israel, "the man after God's own heart" had become David the seducer, the adulterer, the liar, the killer, utterly pitiless and unmoved by his monstrous misdeeds. Israel's ruler was now ruled by sin. He had discovered the truth of Augustine's axiom: "The punishment for sin is sin."

Eventually, David had to face the facts. To be more precise, he had to face the prophet Nathan, who dug up the facts. Nathan trapped the shepherd-king with a trumped-up story about a rich man who had vast flocks of sheep but who seized another man's pet lamb to serve to a "traveling stranger," Nathan's metaphor for David's transient passion (2 Samuel 12:14).

David was enraged: "As surely as the LORD lives, the man who did this deserves to die! He must pay for that lamb four times over, because he did such a thing and had no pity" (12:5). Sheepnapping was not a capital offense in Israel. According to Israelite law a thief was only required to make fourfold restitution to the victim (Exodus 22:1). David was over-reacting out of moral outrage: What monstrous cruelty!

Nathan drove his verdict home. "You are the man! This is what the LORD, the God of Israel, says: 'I anointed you king over Israel, and I delivered you from the hand of Saul. I gave your master's house to you, and your master's wives into your arms. I gave you the house of Israel and Judah. And if all this had been too little I would have given you more. Why did you despise the word of the LORD by doing what is evil in his eyes?" (12:7–9).

Brought face to face with his corruption, David's defenses crumbled. Burying his face in his hands, he cried, "I have sinned against the LORD." And Nathan replied, "The LORD has also taken away your sin. You are not going to die" (12:13).

To David's credit he did not try to justify himself. He acknowledged his sin, and God immediately canceled the handwriting that was against him. David could lift up his head. As he later wrote (Psalm 32:5):

> I acknowledged my sin to you,
> > and did not cover up my iniquity.
> I said, "I will confess
> > my transgression to the LORD"—
> and you forgave
> > the guilt of my sin.

As John promised, "If we confess [acknowledge] our sins, he is faithful and just and will forgive us our sins and purify us from *all* unrighteousness" (1 John 1:9). Happiness is knowing that our sins have been forgiven.

> Blessed [happy] is he
> > whose transgressions are forgiven,
> > whose sins are covered.
> Blessed [happy] is the man
> > whose sin the LORD does not count against him
> > and in whose spirit is no deceit (Psalm 32:1–2).

David bore terrible consequences for his sin. Nathan predicted that he would suffer:

> The sword shall never depart from your house, because you despised me and took the wife of Uriah the Hittite to be your own.
> > This is what the LORD says: "Out of your own household I am going to bring calamity upon you. Before

your very eyes I will take your wives and give them to one who is close to you, and he will lie with your wives in broad daylight. You did it in secret, but I will do this thing in broad daylight before all Israel. . . . Because by doing this you have made the enemies of the LORD show utter contempt, the son born to you will die"
(2 Samuel 12:10–12, 14).

David paid dearly for his few moments of pleasure. His family life and political career fell apart at the seams from that time on.

His oldest son Amnon raped his younger half-sister Tamar. Absalom, who was David's heir apparent, murdered Amnon in retaliation.

Absalom rebelled against David and drove him from the throne, and then, as a sign of disdain for his father, lay with his wives—in broad daylight on the roof of David's house where everyone could see it (2 Samuel 16:20–22). He did so at the advice of David's embittered counselor, Ahithophel, who never forgot what David had done to his dear granddaughter, Bathsheba, and her husband, Uriah.

Absalom himself, who despite his disloyalty remained David's favorite son, was brutally killed by one of David's soldiers.

And finally, as Nathan had predicted, the little boy born of David's affair with Bathsheba, who in a short time had wound his way around David's heart, died suddenly.

God cannot be mocked. Whatever a man sows that shall he reap (Galatians 6:7).

But David could rise from his fall to walk with God. "No amount of falls will really undo us," wrote C. S. Lewis, "if we keep picking ourselves up each time. We shall of course be very muddy and tattered children by the time we reach home. . . . The only fatal thing is to lose one's temper and give up."

The Law of Inevitable Sequence

Reading David's story and watching my friends fall has led me to one conclusion: Moral collapse is rarely a blowout; it's more like a slow leak—the result of a thousand small indulgences. Hardly anyone plans an adulterous affair: they transition into it.

It begins with attraction. It's not so much lust as infatuation that brings us down. We find ourselves drawn to someone sensitive and understanding, someone who listens well and seems to care. We're seduced by that attraction and led on by subtle degrees.

Attraction becomes fantasy: We imagine ourselves with that person and the feeling is good. Fictionalized affairs always seem so right. That's their fundamental deception.

The fantasies soften us and our convictions erode. We're then in a frame of mind to listen to our longings, and having listened we have no will to resist. We cannot escape the realization of our predominate thoughts (Proverbs 23:7).

Then there are the meeting, the sharing of inner conflict, marital disappointment, and other deep hurts, and with that sharing the relationship begins to shift: We're suddenly two lonely people in need of one another's love.

Then comes the inevitable yielding and with that yielding the need to justify the affair. We can't live with the dissonance. We have to rationalize our behavior by blaming someone or something else—the pressures of our business or the limitations of our spouses. Other's wrong-doing becomes our reason. Everything must be made to look good.

But our hearts know. There are moments when our wills soften and we long to set things right. If we do not then listen to our hearts, there comes a metallic hardening, and then corruption. Our wrongdoing mutates, altering its form and quality, evolving into dark narcissism and horrifying cruelty; we don't care who gets hurt as long as we get what we want.

And finally there is inevitable disclosure. First we deny: "There's no one else!" Then we dissemble: "It's only platonic." And finally our deception is shouted from the housetops. There's no place to hide from the light.

When our seams have been opened, when our evil deeds have been exposed, then God reminds us of his cross, his forgiveness, and his incomparable grace and begins to make us new. But there's only one way to know that forgiveness: acknowledgment of the awfulness of one's sin and that old-fashioned word, *repentance*. We must hate what we've done, and turn from it in disgust.

That's what Paul calls "godly sorrow [that] brings repentance that leads to salvation and leaves no regret" (2 Corinthians 7:10). Ungodly sorrow is the sorrow of being found out, or of suffering the consequences of being found out. The result is intensified guilt, anxiety, and hopelessness. Godly sorrow, on the other hand, is sorrow over sin itself and the harm that it's done to others. Godly sorrow asserts itself to set things right.

Here's the way Paul put it: "See what this godly sorrow has produced in you: what earnestness [to obey], what eagerness to clear yourselves [of wrongdoing], what indignation [against evil], what alarm [that we might fall into sin again], what longing [for purity], what concern [for all those damaged by our sin], what readiness to see justice [righteousness] done" (2 Corinthians 7:11).

As David himself learned, "The sacrifice of God is a broken spirit; a broken and contrite heart you will not despise" (Psalm 51:17). God discerns the possibilities even in our defilement, unmakes the mistakes, and sets out to make us better than we've ever been before.

He uses our sin to awaken our need for his grace, and he softens us and makes us more susceptible to his shaping than we've ever been before. When we fall, we have fallen into his arms. As one of George MacDonald's characters said, "When a man or woman repents an' humbles himsel', there [God] is to lift them up—an' higher than they ever stood afore!"

Therefore, rather than mourn our humiliation we must move on. Sin may have consequences with which we must live for the rest of our natural lives, but sin repented of can only work for ultimate good. God takes the worst that we can do and makes it part of the good he has promised. He's the God of fools and failures and the God of another chance.

Avoiding the inevitable

Anyone can fall. The main thing is to know how vulnerable we are and *always* be on the alert. We're overthrown because we're unguarded (1 Corinthians 10:12). "What can we do?" we ask.

We can guard our relationship with God. The wise man says, "Above all else, guard your heart, for it is the wellspring of life" (Proverbs 4:23). There's a close relationship between human sexuality and human spirituality. Charles Williams observed, "Sensuality and sanctity are so closely intertwined that our motives in some cases can hardly be separated until the tares are gathered out of the wheat by heavenly wit."

Sexual passion is in some inexplicable way a small representation of our more profound, spiritual passion for God—our "urge to merge" with him. He alone can gratify that desire. Devotion to Christ serves to satisfy our deepest longings and quell our other lusts. But when our love for Christ is on the wane, we get restless for something more and our resolve in every area begins to weaken.

John Donne wrote,

> *Take me to You, imprison me, for I,*
> *Except You enthrall me, never shall be free,*
> *Nor ever chaste, except you ravish me.*

Another early Christian, Saint Anthony (A.D. 251–356) wrote, "The devil can in no way enter our mind or body unless he has first deprived it of all holy thoughts and made it empty and bare of spiritual contemplation."

We can guard our minds against romantic and sexual fantasies. Our predominant thoughts determine our inevitable actions; what we think in our hearts is what we eventually, inevitably do.

"But," you ask, "how can we stop our erotic thoughts?" Philip Melanchthon lamented, "Old Adam is much too strong for young Philip!" Indeed. Our fantasies are much too strong to subordinate. We should rather re-channel them or displace them. When sexual fantasies intrude into our thoughts we have two choices: We can reinforce them, in which case they eventually become obsession; or we can sidetrack them into devotion, meditation, and prayer (see Philippians 4:8).

We can cultivate affection for our spouses, daily rekindling the love and passion of our marriages, maintaining its romance. That's mutual protection (Proverbs 5:15–20). We're terribly vulnerable if we neglect our marriages, permitting them to grow dull and unfriendly.

We can keep our hands to ourselves. "It is touch that is the deadliest enemy of chastity, loyalty, monogamy . . . ," Wallace Stegner wrote. "By touch we are betrayed and betray others."

We can watch for infatuations. Augustine confessed that he could not distinguish between the "clear shining of affection and the darkness of lust." Further, he admitted, I could not keep myself within the kingdom of light where friendship binds soul to soul. . . . And so I polluted the brook of friendship with the sewage of lust."

Are we attracted to someone other than our spouse? Do we look forward to being with them? Do we look for excuses to meet them? Do we dress a certain way when we know we will be with that person? Do we find ourselves wanting to reach out and touch them, hug them, or express affection in tender ways? Do we imagine a romantic or sexual relationship them? Are we defensive when our spouses express uneasiness about our relationship with that person? These are early warning signs of a friendship turning into infatuation.

St. Francis de Sales said, "We must be on guard against deception in friendships, especially when they are contracted between persons of different sexes, no matter what the pretext may be. Satan often tricks those [who] begin with virtuous love. If they are not very prudent, fond love will first be injected, next sensual love, and then carnal love. . . . [Satan] does this subtly and tries to introduce impurity by insensible degrees."

We can guard against intimacy with anyone other than our mates. The secrets of our hearts, our deepest hurts and longings, are reserved for them alone. The greatest mistake we can make is to share our inner conflict and marital disappointment with someone of the opposite sex.

We can be alert during periods of unusual pressure. Flaws always show up under stress. We should be especially wary on days when we're emotionally and physically depleted, when we are lonely and isolated and longing for attention and affirmation.

We can guard ourselves against those who come after us. Occasionally a man will encounter a lonely hunter, dressed for the kill and with "crafty intent" (Proverbs 7:10). And there are those male conquistadors, who spend their energies preying on women. Such people, though they may not know it, exist to bring others down (see Proverbs 5:1–23 and 7:1–27).

We can regularly rehearse the consequences of an affair. We gain insight through hindsight, as someone has said, but foresight is the less costly way. As Proverbs warns us, though "the lips of an adulteress drip honey and her speech is smoother than oil; [make no mistake] in the end she is bitter as gall, sharp as a double-edged sword. Her feet go down to death; her steps lead straight to the grave" (Proverbs 5:3–5). Adultery is suicide; the victim is your soul.

Paul Dunbar wrote,

> *This is the debt I pay*
> *Just for one riotous day,*
> *Years of regret and grief,*
> *Sorrow without relief.*
>
> *Slight was the thing I bought,*
> *Small was the debt I thought,*
> *Poor was the loan at best—*
> *God! but the interest!*

Years ago a friend of mine received a note from a man who had been involved in an affair and whose marriage had crumbled. This is what he wrote: "I have to live the rest of my life now without the person I truly love and that used to love me, with no chance to undo the wrong I've committed. I lost the best thing that ever happened to me—my best friend."

We can publicize our home life, talk lovingly of our spouses, and surround ourselves with momentos, pictures, and reminders of our marriages. It's good for us and it's good for others; it lets them know we cherish our mates.

We can find a friend on whom we can unload our darkest secrets, who will not flinch when they hear the sordid stuff of our minds, who will hold a confidence, who will hold us accountable, who will ask us the tough questions and then ask, "Did you lie?" (Men and women in trouble lie.)

We can ask God to guard us every minute of the day. Every man has his price; every one of us can fall at any time. We say, "There, but for the grace of God, I might have gone." Better: "There, but for the grace of God, I may yet go."

We're in terrible danger whether we're young or old, single or married, in the dumps or on a roll. We're fools if we think we cannot fall. We're frail and unfinished. No matter how willing the spirit, the flesh will always be weak. Our safety doesn't lie in keeping ourselves safe, but in putting ourselves in God's hands for safekeeping.

Jesus' words sound the best advice: "Watch and pray so that you will not fall into temptation" (Matthew 26:41).

WHEN PEOPLE THROW STONES

This must be your retaliation—love and truth for hatred and lies.

—Rudolph Stier

A man once told me that I was a "wicked shepherd who was destroying and scattering the sheep." Those were his very words.

I asked him if he knew that he was quoting scripture. He said he did. I asked him if he knew by whom it was said and about whom. He did not. I told him it was the prophet Jeremiah who said it (23:1) and that it was said about each of Judah's last four kings: Zedekiah, Shallum, Jehoiakim, and Coniah, four of the worst men who ever lived (23:1). I thought that would change his mind, but it didn't.

The best of life is swallowed up by the worst, and sometimes the worst comes in the form of mean-spirited attacks on our character. Yet, even heartless censure can be redemptive. God uses the worst that men can say about us to shape our character and strengthen us. An incident in the Old Testament illustrates the reality of this truth: the story of Shimei, the mean-spirited little man who threw rocks at David (2 Samuel 16:5–14 NASB).

Shimei and his kin

The book of 2 Samuel is about David—his fortunes and misfortunes. David was a brilliant and far-sighted leader, and, more importantly, he was a man with a heart for God; but he had almost constant trouble with his family. His wives and children repeatedly caused him grief. The background for this story is another instance of family dysfunction: the rebellion of Absalom, his son.

The trouble began when Absalom's sister, Tamar, was raped and humiliated by Amnon, another of David's sons. David did nothing. Absalom waited for two years before taking matters into his own hands by murdering his brother and fleeing into exile in Syria (2 Samuel 13:20–29). He was later forgiven by David and allowed to return, but soon after he began plotting to seize the throne.

Absalom devoted four years preparing for a takeover, currying favor with the people and setting up his agents throughout the kingdom (15:1–12). Then, his plans laid, he went to Hebron, gathered the people, engineered his own anointing as king, and marched on Jerusalem with his army.

When the report of Absalom's revolt came to David, he was taken completely by surprise. He had either minimized Absalom's strategy or was unaware of it. "David said to all his servants who were with him at Jerusalem, 'Arise and let us flee, for otherwise none of us shall escape from Absalom. Go in haste, lest he overtake us quickly and bring down calamity on us and strike the city with the edge of the sword' " (2 Samuel 15:14 NASB).

David was not a coward. His flight was not motivated by fear, but by the tactics of warfare. He knew he would be pinned down in the city. So to spare Jerusalem the horrors of a siege and to gain time for his friends to gather, he withdrew.

"The king went out and all the people with him, and they stopped at the last house. Now all his servants passed on beside him, all the Cherethites, all the Pelethites, and all the Gittites, [his personal bodyguard] six hundred men who had come with him from Gath passed on before the king" (15:17–18 NASB).

David felt one blow after another, calamities fell on him like bricks tumbling from a dump truck. He had to send Zadok, his priest and pastor, back to Jerusalem; he discovered that his trusted friend and wise counselor, Ahithophel, was a traitor; he sent his loyal, aged friend, Hushai, back to Jerusalem; and he was told by Ziba that Saul's grandson, Mephibosheth, to whom David had shown such kindness, was among the conspirators.

Then, "when King David came to Bahurim, behold, there came out from there a man of the family of the house of Saul whose name was Shimei, the son of Gera; he came out cursing continually as he came" (16:5 NASB).

Bahurim was a small village a few miles from Jerusalem on the road to Jericho. As David approached the city, Shimei, one of Saul's descendants and a man who shared Saul's hostility to the House of David, came out cursing him and pelting him with rocks. "He threw stones at David and at all the servants of King David; and all the people and all the mighty men were at his right hand and at his left" (16:6 NASB). (The intensive form of the verb translated "threw" suggests that he was gunning each rock in!) David's bodyguards anxiously gathered around to shield him.

"Thus Shimei said when he cursed, 'Get out, get out, you man of bloodshed [murderer], and worthless fellow [trash]! The LORD has returned upon you all the bloodshed of the house of Saul, in whose place you have reigned; and the LORD has given the kingdom into the hand of your son Absalom. And behold, you are taken in your own evil, for you are a man of bloodshed!' " (16:7–8).

Shimei's charge was unfounded. Saul's life had been in David's hands more than once, but he had refused to touch "the Lord's anointed," as David put it, even though Saul ruthlessly pursued him and tried to put him to death. David executed the man who later killed Saul and put to death those who assassinated Saul's son, Ishbosheth. He wept for Saul and his son Jonathan when they fell at Gilboa, and composed a beautiful and poignant poem about these two brave men (2 Samuel 1:19–27), and then he took Mephibosheth, Jonathan's son, into his own home. He was totally innocent of Shimei's charge.

"Then Abishai the son of Zeruiah said to the king, 'Why should this dead dog curse my lord the king? Let me go over, and cut off his head" (16:9 NASB). Abishai was David's nephew, one of his hot tempered young retainers, fiercely loyal to the king. He was protective of his uncle, and on at least one occasion had saved his life (2 Samuel 21:16–17). His violence was legendary (2 Samuel 23:18–19).

But David restrained him:

> The king said, "What have I to do with you, O sons of Zeruiah? If he curses, and if the LORD has told him, 'Curse David,' then who shall say, 'Why have you done so?' "
>
> David then said to Abishai and to all his officials, "My son, who is of my own flesh, is trying to take my life. How much more, then, this Benjamite! Leave him alone; let him curse, for the LORD has told him to. It may be that the LORD will see my distress and repay me with good for the cursing I am receiving today."

So David and his men continued along the road while Shimei was going along the hillside opposite him, cursing as he went and throwing stones at him and showering him with dirt. The king and all the people with him arrived at their destination exhausted. And there he refreshed himself" (16:10–14).

Shimei followed David and his entourage to Bahurim where David and his men stopped to rest. It's probable that he continued to molest the camp, raving and cursing into the night, but David was able to refresh himself there.

We're told later that when David returned to Jerusalem after putting down Absalom's revolt, Shimei met the returning king at the fords of the Jordan and begged for mercy (2 Samuel 19:15–23). David forgave him but later warned Solomon of his treachery. He was not a man to be trusted. Finally, Solomon put Shimei to death, but David never avenged himself on this spiteful little man.

Shimei then and now

As I have thought about Shimei and my own critics, several judgments have formed in my mind. For instance, criticism always seems to come when we need it least.

David had been driven from his city, separated from his family, betrayed by this best friends, and targeted by his own son. He was already in the dumps when Shimei began his attack. *Who needs it?* he must have thought.

Criticism rarely comes when we're up and on top of things. It's usually when we're down and out that some critic comes along. People pile judgments on our sorrow and suffering, and once they get going, they can't seem to stop.

Also, it seems to me, the worst critiques come when we least deserve them. David wasn't always right, but on this occasion he was innocent of any wrongdoing. He didn't deserve Shimei's curses. But we shouldn't be surprised. "Evil is always more readily spoken of and believed of another than good," said Thomas à Kempis.

And then it has been my experience that criticism usually comes from people who are least qualified to give it. Much of it is generated by people who don't know what they're talking about, or who are so morally unqualified they have no right to throw stones. Like Shimei. They have no heart for God or for God's plan to bring salvation to the world. Yet it is often from these people we receive the harshest blows.

And finally, criticism often comes in a form that is least helpful. It's hard enough to take a critique when it comes in love, but no one likes to hear it when it's hard and harsh—when our character and motives are assailed. It would be good if all our critics were gentle and redemptive, but that's often not the case. Sometimes they just like to throw rocks.

The name of the game

The wisest of souls have always warned us not to expect too much of people. Jesus assures us that "no one who has left home or brothers or sisters or mother or father or children or fields for me and the gospel will fail to receive a hundred times as much in this present age—*and with them, persecutions*" (Mark 10:29–30).

Paul agrees: "Everyone who wants to live a godly life in Christ Jesus *will be persecuted*" (2 Timothy 3:12). *Everyone* who sets out to follow the Lord will be criticized, opposed, and misunderstood. Every step of the journey will be contested; every decision will be tested and challenged.

The only way to avoid reproach is to determine to be nothing, do nothing, and say nothing. Charles Briggs wrote, "If your ambition is to avoid the troubles of life, the recipe is simple: shed your ambitions in every direction, cut the wings of every soaring purpose, and seek a little life with the fewest contacts and relations. . . . Tiny souls can dodge through life; bigger souls are blocked on every side. As soon as men and women begin to enlarge their lives, their resistances are multiplied." To be significant is to be misunderstood.

Handling the hard shots

Something needs to be said to critics: lighten up. But something also needs to be said to the criticized: toughen up.

Our critics may hurt us profoundly, but we mustn't let them deter us. "Even though much provoked," Abraham Lincoln said in the face of intense and cruel criticism, "let us do nothing through passion and ill temper . . . neither let us be slandered from our duty by false accusations against ourselves. . . . Let us have faith and in that faith let us to the end dare to do our duty as we understand it."

"The Lord has told him"

The first step in toughening up is to acknowledge God's hand in the matter. David said of Shimei's ruthless rock-throwing, "Let him alone and let him curse, for the LORD has told him . . . ." (2 Samuel 16:11). David clearly saw God's hand in the matter. There are no secondary causes. As the Heidelberg Catechism puts it, "All things . . . come to us not by chance but by God's hand."

Criticism may be God's voice dealing with some sin in us that must be dealt with before we can move on. He may be speaking through our worst critics, pointing out some carnality or stupidity in us. "Truth is truth," George MacDonald said, "whether it's spoken by the lips of Jesus or Balaam's ass." Though our critics are speaking we must listen to God's voice. He may be speaking through our worst enemies, pointing out some wrong in us.

"Consider the source," we say. No, consider the criticism, especially if it comes from more than one person. An old

Yiddish proverb says, "If one man calls you an ass, pay him no mind. If two men call you an ass, go buy a saddle."

There may be more truth in our enemies' words than in the counsel of our friends. Perhaps their eyes are sharper than our friends' eyes, or our friends may be aware of our weakness and unwilling to tell us. Love is quick to note our faults, but sometimes slow to point them out and correct them. The highest love always girds itself for the task of washing our feet, but it's a dirty job and one our friends are reluctant to do.

Spurgeon said, "Get your friend to tell you your faults, or better still, welcome an enemy who will watch you keenly and sting you savagely. What a blessing such an irritating critic will be to a wise man. What an intolerable nuisance to a fool."

> *We learn from our friends,*
> *But heaven knows,*
> *The lasting lessons*
> *come from our foes.*

> **—Pat D'Amico**

When there is an element of truth in a rebuke, we must be willing to hear it and deal with the sin involved. David said, "Let the righteous smite me in loving kindness. It is oil on my head. Do not let me refuse it" (Psalm 141:5).

We should search our hearts to see if the criticism is true before dismissing it or treating it with disdain. Before we tear up that searing note, or reject that harsh comment we should present ourselves before our Lord's gentle presence and ask ourselves if we can honestly say we are blameless.

We should listen carefully and consider what's being said, giving the Holy Spirit adequate time to impress it upon us. We may respond by asking for time to think about what has been said. Then if we are truly convinced of our sin we should immediately confess it before God and before those we have wronged.

We should not delay. As Jesus said "Settle matters *quickly* with your adversary" (Matthew 5:25). And again, "Therefore, if you are offering your gift at the altar and there remember that your brother has something against you, leave your gift there in front of the altar. First go and be reconciled to your brother; then come and offer your gift" (Matthew 5:23).

Some people will not be satisfied with any confession, no matter how genuine. They cannot forgive and forget, and they will not believe that our repentance is sincere. They endlessly process past sins and their pain, and they cannot let go and move on. It's hard to let such issues remain unresolved, but we must do so. We will always receive more mercy from God than we will from men and women. David prayed, "Let us fall into the hands of the LORD, for his mercy is great; but do not let me fall into the hands of men" (2 Samuel 24:14).

If there is no basis for reproach, give thanks. We should be grateful that God has kept us from actual sin, and we should thank him for his empowering grace. We might have committed that sin or worse!

Ultimately, no criticism is undeserved. Though we may not be guilty of the sin of which we're accused, in one way or another, small or great, hidden or revealed, we are sinful to the core.

Boris Kornfield, the physician who led Alexander Solzhenitsyn to Christ, wrote, "On the whole, I have become convinced that there is no punishment that comes to us in this life on earth which is undeserved. Superficially, it can have nothing to do with what we are guilty of in actual fact, but if you go over your life with a fine tooth comb and ponder it deeply, you will always be able to hunt down that transgression of yours for which you have now received this blow."

But what of those malicious people who are out to hang us? Is it God's will that they be unleashed? Indeed! Even when the criticism is cruel it will do us good to hear it because we must learn to endure hatred. Our Lord was nailed to the cross. You can count on it that you will be nailed to the wall!

God gives us over to such hurt because it is part of the process to make us what he intends us to be. The hurting makes us sweeter, more mellow. We lose the fear of losing; we learn to let go of what we want. We're not so easily provoked to wrath by harm or reproof. We learn to absorb abuse without retaliation, to accept reproof without defensiveness, to return a soft answer to wrath. It makes us calm and strong.

> *Firm in the right; mild to the wrong*
> *Our heart, in every raging throng*
> *A chamber shut for prayer and song.*

—George MacDonald

Hostility and accusation teach us to pray. David wrote, "In return for my friendship they accuse me, but I am a man of prayer" (Psalm 109:4). The translators supplied "a man of," but the text reads simply, "I am prayer." Prayer became the essence of David's life.

Criticism is a powerful instrument to develop our relationship with God. It moves us closer to him and makes us more susceptible to his shaping. William Law wrote, "Receive every inward and outward trouble, every disappointment, pain, uneasiness, temptation, darkness and despair with both hands as a true opportunity and blessed occasion for dying to self and entering into a fuller fellowship with your self-denying and suffering Savior. Look at no inward or outward trouble with any other view. Reject every other thought about it and then every kind of pain and bitterness will become the blessed day of your prosperity."

Sometimes it is good that we put up with people speaking against us, and sometimes it is good that we be thought of as bad and flawed, even when we do good things and have good intentions. Such troubles are often aids to humility, and they protect us from pride. Indeed, we are sometimes better at seeking God when people have nothing but bad things to say about us and when they refuse to give us credit for the good things we have done! That being the case, we should so root ourselves in God that we do not need to look for comfort anywhere else.

—Thomas à Kempis

We should accept every hostile comment as an opportunity to draw near to God. We should look upon anyone who speaks against us as God's voice saying to us, "Come closer."

Hebrews says we should "consider him who endured such opposition from sinful men, so that [we] will not grow weary and lose heart" (Hebrews 12:3). Jesus knows what it means to be overwhelmed by one's enemies and by one's friends.

In his hour of greatest need, when his soul was "overwhelmed with sorrow to the point of death," he opened his heart to his three best friends, Peter and the two sons of Zebedee, and asked them to stay with him and pray. They fell asleep. "Could you men not keep watch with me for one hour?" he lamented. What poignancy! And then in the end, his friends "forsook him and fled" (see Matthew 26:26–56).

So, when our friends fail to come through, when no one supports us, when no one calls or drops by to ask how we're doing, when there are no cards or letters, no cheery notes of comfort, we know our Lord knows and cares.

A portion of Psalm 4 speaks to our deepest need at such times:

How long, O men, will you turn my glory into shame?
How long will you love delusions and seek false
gods?
Know that the LORD has set apart the godly for
himself;
the LORD will hear when I call to him (Psalm
4:2–3).

David was concerned about the rising tide of disloyalty in
his nation. His authority was being undermined. He was in
the minority, always an uncomfortable place to be, but more
so when the minority is shrinking. Nevertheless, David
insists, "The LORD has set apart the godly for himself."

"Godly" sounds daunting since we associate the word
with awesome piety, but the term simply refers to those that
have chosen to be loyal to God alone. Rabbi Kimchi wrote,
"The *kasid* [the godly man] is the man whom God loves and
who loves God."

People make up fantasies and tell lies about us, but the
Lord has set us apart for himself. He chooses us for his own
enjoyment. Out of the many there are the few with whom he
can commune. They are those whom criticism and blame
have brought to their knees. Hatred, hurt, and stings of
indifference are all part of the process by which God weans
us away from earthly attachments and worldly ambition and
brings us to the place that we look to him alone for our
approval—where we say with David, "You *alone*, O LORD,
make me dwell in safety" (Psalm 4:8).

That's worth everything in the world.

Strength under control

I take great comfort in the psalmist's words,

Do not fret because of evil men, or be envious of
those who do wrong;

for like the grass they will soon wither, like green
    plants they will soon die away.
Trust in the LORD and do good; dwell in the land and
    enjoy safe pasture.
Delight yourself in the LORD and he will give you the
    desires of your heart.
Commit your way to the LORD; trust in him and he
    will do this:
He will make your righteousness shine like the dawn,
    the justice of your cause like the noonday sun.
Be still before the LORD and wait patiently for him; do
    not fret when men succeed in their ways,
    when they carry out their wicked schemes.
Refrain from anger and turn from wrath; do not fret—
    it leads only to evil.
For evil men will be cut off, but those who hope in the
    LORD will inherit the land.
A little while, and the wicked will be no more; though
    you look for them, they will not be found.
But the meek will inherit the land and enjoy great
    peace (Psalm 37:1–11).

Meekness is not weakness, but strength under control. It
is a refusal to defend ourselves or to retaliate against
wrong—to be humble, non-defensive, and unassuming in the
face of brutal and heartless attack. There is a wonderful sense
of the Father's approval and affection when we lay down our
lives in this way. Jesus said, "My Father loves me because I
lay down my life" (John 10:17).

Remember Peter's words, "Christ also suffered for you,
leaving you an example for you to follow in His steps, who
committed no sin, nor was any deceit found in his mouth; and
while being reviled, he did not revile in return; while
suffering, he uttered no threats, but kept entrusting himself to
Him who judges righteously" (1 Peter 2:21–23). Jesus did not

repay the world's curses and blows. He waited for the Father to defend him.

One church father, Justin Martyr, said, "Jesus' greatest miracle is that he did not retaliate." When our Lord's turn came and he was stretched out on the cross, instead of bitter resentment against his executioners he offered up his life to God and waited for his vindication. That was the secret of his composure and ours.

With Augustine we should pray again and again, "Heal me of this lust of mine of always vindicating myself." Why do we smart under others' criticisms? Why do we care so much what others say about us? Is it because we place too much value on our own reputations and the favor and the appreciation of men? Do we have a terrible fear of being despised and rejected?

A. W. Tozer writes, "The labor of self-love is a heavy one indeed. Think of yourself whether much of your sorrow has not arisen from someone speaking slightingly of you. As long as you set yourself up as a little god to which you must be loyal there will be those who will delight to offer affront to your idol. How then can you hope to have inward peace? The heart's fierce effort to protect itself from every slight, to shield its touchy honor from the bad opinion of friend and enemy, will never let the mind have rest."

We're God's servants. If he is satisfied with us, why should we break our hearts over what others say? The Lord of the church has chosen us and put us into the positions we enjoy. He is our judge, and if he is pleased with us there is nothing anyone can say or do that can ever dissuade him.

"Let them talk," Alexander Whyte said. "Let them write; let them correct you; let them traduce you; let them judge and condemn you; let them slay you. . . . Oh the detestable passions that corrections and contradictions kindle up to fury in the proud heart of man! Eschew controversy as you would eschew the entrance into hell itself. Let them have their way."

We may ask our opponent to justify his charges, or, if the charges are false, we can meet them with steadfast denial. Truth spoken to establish the truth is not defensiveness. Nehemiah, when accused of falsehood and shifty motives simply replied, "Nothing like what you are saying is happening" (Nehemiah 6:8). But if they will not believe us we must "let the turbid stream of rumor flow" and wait for our Father's "well done."

Paul says, "I care very little if I am judged by you or by any human court; indeed I do not even judge myself . . . . It is the Lord who judges me" (1 Corinthians 4:3–4). God is the only one who can properly evaluate the quality of our lives. He knows all the latent forces underlying our behavior as well as the patent facts that others see. When we are unjustly criticized we should remember that he knows us as no one else does. As A. J. Cronin's much-maligned priest, Father Chisolm, said with such calm simplicity, "I shall render an account of my life to God."

"The Lord will look on my affliction"

For whom the heart of man shuts out;
the heart of God shuts in.

—F. B. Meyer

"Perhaps the Lord will look on my affliction and return good to me instead of his cursing this day," David said (2 Samuel 16:12 NASB).

We must take every criticism to our Advocate and let him vindicate us: "He stands at the right hand of the needy to save him from those who judge his soul" (Psalm 109:31 NASB).

God knows what others are saying about us and it grieves him deeply. He has considered every angle; he has taken every factor into account. In time he will take our side.

F. B. Meyer writes, "Whenever an affront or wrong is inflicted on thee, avoid vindicating, or answering for thyself. Be still towards man, unless it be to induce thy brother to repent; but turn instantly to thy righteous Judge, asking him to right the wrong and vindicate the right. He shall bring forth thy righteousness as the light, and thy judgment as noonday. When Christians go to law, and seek to maintain their cause against wrong-doing they miss this. The weaker you are, the more certainly will God judge for you."

There is an old Quaker saying, "If we fight the beast by becoming a beast then bestiality has won." Paul says, "Do not take revenge, my friends, but leave room for God's wrath, for it is written: 'It is mine to avenge; I will repay,' says the Lord" (Romans 12:19).

When we have done all we can do, the only thing left is to wait patiently until God avenges the wrong and vindicates us. God will refute our critics in his own time and way—in this life or in the next. God is the Alpha and Omega. He and not our accusers will have the last word. It may be that our enemies will find out then that we are not so much to blame as they thought.

God is aware of every factor and has pondered every angle of our circumstances. Why do we say, "My way is hidden from the LORD my cause is disregarded by my God?"

> Do you not know?
> > Have you not heard?
> The LORD is the everlasting God,
> > the Creator of the ends of the earth.
> He will not grow tired or weary, and his understanding
> > no one can fathom.
> He gives strength to the weary and increases the power
> > of the weak.
> Even youths grow tired and weary, and young men
> > stumble and fall;

but those who hope in the LORD will renew their strength.
They will soar on wings like eagles;
> they will run and not grow weary,
> they will walk and not be faint (Isaiah 40:28–31).

God "loves justice" (Psalm 11:7). In his time and in his way he will set everything right. He stands between us and our enemies; he will not leave us in their hands. He acts firmly and no one can interfere. In the meantime, we are shadowed and sheltered under his wings. No one can hinder or harm us there.

God says insistently and strongly, "They will fight against you, but they will not overcome you, for I am with you and will rescue you" (Jeremiah 1:19). He does not say you will not be assaulted, belabored, or disquieted. He says you will not be overcome. "Nothing in life is quite so exhilarating," Winston Churchill chortled, "as being shot at without result."

Knowing that God has taken up our cause enables us to be nondefensive. The weak have to defend their dignity and rights. Those who are strengthened by God can yield. "Let your forbearance be evident to all," Paul writes, "The Lord is near" (Philippians 4:5).

St. John of the Cross says that those who are guarded by God have three distinguishing characteristics—tranquillity, gentleness, and strength. Anxiety, intensity, instability, and pessimism plague us when we try to protect ourselves, but those who are shielded and strengthened by God share the calm and quiet nature of the One in whom they trust.

> *The wind of words may toss my heart,*
> > *But what is that to me!*
> *'Tis but a surface storm—Thou art*
> > *My deep, still resting sea.*

So if my heart with trouble now
Be throbbing in my breast
Thou art my deepest heart, and Thou
O God, dost ever rest.

—George MacDonald

"Father forgive them . . ."

Don't worry if people mock you, malign you, tell lies about you. Don't worry if they turn on you. Just don't turn on them. Ask God to give you the grace to tolerate those who grieve you.

We must never nourish thoughts of hatred or retaliation. We should rather think of the misery of our enemies hearts—full as they are of jealousy, envy, and bitterness. We must pity them and pray for them.

Jesus said, "Love your enemies, do good to those who hate you, bless those who curse you, pray for those who mistreat you" (Luke 6:27). Love, generosity, blessing, and intercessory prayer are the gifts we have to give to those who revile us.

Consider Judas. Though our Lord knew from the beginning who would betray him, not one of his disciples knew (John 13:22). Nothing in Jesus' behavior betrayed the betrayer.

Jesus prayed from the cross, "Father forgive them . . . ," not when the crucifixion was over, and men were sorry for what they did, but in the very moment it was being done. So it must be us. "To see that my adversary gives me my rights is natural," Oswald Chambers writes, "but from our Lord's standpoint it does not matter if I am defrauded or not; what does matter is that I do not defraud."

We must go beyond forgiveness to tender love, concerned more with the misery of the person from which the criticism came than our own misery, showing our critics mercy, serving them, praying earnestly for them, refusing to wrong them or withdraw from them, taking their wrongs as God takes ours. Brooding over wrong keeps the wounds open. Only forgiveness heals.

> *O give us hearts to love like Thee*
> *Like Thee, O Lord, to grieve*
> *Far more for others' sins than all*
> *The wrongs that we receive.*

—Author unknown

Impossible? "Nothing is impossible with God" (Luke 1:37). We should pray as George MacDonald prayed: "O God, make me into a rock which swallows up the waves of wrong in its great caverns and never throws them back to swell the commotion of the angry sea from whence they came. Ah! To annihilate wrong in this way—to say, 'It shall not be wrong against me, so utterly do I forgive it!' "

This is the majesty of meekness: to bear patiently the spiteful attacks of malice and envy; to overcome evil with good; to live in the midst of difficult people and love them; to keep our mouths closed and our hearts open when we're in the presence of our critics; to be unruffled and composed through a storm of unkindness and misrepresentation; "to let the turbid stream of rumor flow thro' either babbling world high or low . . . to never speak against a foe" (F. B. Meyer).

This is only possible to those "in whose breast the dove-like Spirit has found an abiding place, and whose hearts are guarded by the peace of God. These are those who bear themselves as heroes in the fight" (Oswald Chambers).

Aftermath

The end of the story of David and Shimei is Psalm 3, the poem David wrote that night:

O LORD, how many are my foes!
    How many rise up against me!
Many are saying of me,
    "God will not deliver him."

But you are a shield around me, O LORD;
    you bestow glory on me and lift up my
        head.
To the LORD I cry aloud,
    and he answers me from his holy hill.

I lie down and sleep . . . .

David gave Shimei and all his detractors to God, zipped up his sleeping bag, fluffed up his pillow, rolled over, and went to sleep.

FAILING
SUCCESSFULLY

Those whom God loves he sends failure early.

—Peter Drucker

Jack Staddon of Great Bend, Kansas, won the National Geographic spelling bee several years ago and a $25,000 college scholarship for his efforts. He alone could spell the "flat intermountain area located at 10,000 feet in the Andes" (Altoplano).

"It's nice to win," Jack remarked later, "but even if I lost, I'd thank the Lord anyway. It gives you practice in knowing how to fail."

When failing and succeeding are at issue, an incident in David's life comes to mind. It took place during a period when he and Saul were playing a deadly game of hide and seek. Saul, pursuing David and his band of men in the Judean wilderness, was bent on running him into the ground.

Saul was familiar with all David's haunts and hiding places. David could run but he knew he could not hide. He was weary and worn out. There seemed to be no end to his troubles.

The songs that are assigned to this period of David's life are sad songs. The overriding mood is one of dreary depression and despair.

> Why, O LORD, do you stand far off?
>> Why do you hide yourself in times of trouble?
> (Psalm 10:1).

> How long, O LORD? Will you forget me for ever?
>> How long will you hide your face from me?
> (Psalm 13:1).

> My God, my God, why have you forsaken me?
>> Why are you so far from saving me,
>> so far from the words of my groaning?
> (Psalm 22:1).

David had reached the end of his rope. He just couldn't take it any more.

> [He] thought to himself, "One of these days I shall be
> destroyed by the hand of Saul. The best thing I can do
> is to escape to the land of the Philistines. Then Saul
> will give up searching for me anywhere in Israel, and
> I will slip out of his hand" (1 Samuel 27:1).

In the past David talked to Gad or other of his counselors, or better yet, he "inquired of the Lord," but on this occasion David didn't ask the Lord or anyone else. He looked at his circumstances, took counsel of his fears, and fled to Philistia. Under the circumstances, he believed that was the best thing for him to do.

God had instructed David to take a stand in Judah and set up his standard there (22:5). He was safe in the land. David had God's assurance that his destiny was fixed—an assurance confirmed by Samuel, Jonathan, Saul, and the young woman, Abigail:

> The Lord will certainly make a lasting dynasty for my master, because he fights the LORD's battles . . . . Even though someone is pursuing you to take your life, the life of my master will be bound securely in the bundle of the living by the LORD your God. But the lives of your enemies he will hurl away as from the pocket of a sling (25:28–29).

It's impossible for God to lie or forget his covenant. "By immutable pledges his [David's] Almighty Friend had bound himself, seeking to give his much-tried friend strong consolation, if only he would remain within the sheltering walls of the refuge—harbor which these assurances constituted; and it was easier for heaven and earth to pass away than for one jot or tittle of the Divine promises to become invalid," F. B. Meyer wrote.

But David panicked and fled to Philistia.

Haste makes waste

The phrase translated "I shall escape" is put in a way that suggests great haste: "I shall immediately escape." I will do it *now*!

Decisions made when we're down in the dumps or emotionally distraught are exceedingly perilous. We're most vulnerable to bad choices when we're in that state of mind—choices we would never make if we were on top of things. When we're down we inevitably stumble into bad judgment.

I can't help but wonder how many single people have decided in a moment of weariness they can't handle the thought of perpetual loneliness and have saddled themselves with a mate who has made life for them even more miserable? I wonder how many men have walked away from good jobs in fit of momentary frustration and rage and now find themselves hopelessly out of work or working in situations far less desirable? I wonder how many have given up on their marriages when they are at low ebb and have lived to regret that decision. I wonder how many men have walked away from fruitful ministries because of weariness and discouragement?

I read recently an excerpt from the work by Ignatius of Loyola, a sixteenth-century Basque Christian, entitled *The Spiritual Exercises*. He pointed out that there are two conditions in the Christian life. One is consolation, "when the soul is aroused to a love for its Creator and Lord. When faith, hope and charity, and interior joy inspire the soul to peace and quiet in our Lord." The other is desolation, "when there is darkness of soul, turmoil of mind, a strong inclination to earthly things, restlessness resulting from disturbances and temptations leading to loss of faith. We find ourselves apathetic, tepid, sad and separated, as it were, from our Lord."

"In time of desolation," he wrote, "one should never make a change, but stand firm and constant in the resolution and decision which guided him the day before the desolation, or to the decision which he observed in the preceding consolation. For just as the good spirit guides and consoles us in consolation, so in desolation the evil spirit guides and counsels. Following the counsels of this latter spirit, one can never find the correct way to a right decision."

He continues: "Although in desolation we should not change our earlier resolutions, it will be very advantageous to intensify our activity against desolation. This can be done by insisting more on prayer, meditation, examination, and confession." Sometimes the simple things are the holiest things of all. Once again we should listen to F. B. Meyer:

> Never act in a panic; nor allow man to dictate to thee, calm thyself and be still; force thyself into the quiet of thy closet until the pulse beats normally and the scare has ceased to perturb. When thou art most eager to act is the time when thou wilt make the most pitiable mistakes. Do not say in thine heart what thou wilt or wilt not do; but wait upon God until He makes known his way. So long as that way is hidden, it is clear that there is no need of action, and that He accounts Himself responsible for all the results keeping thee where thou art.

And so, we should wait and pray. David eventually learned "to wait for [God] all day long" (Psalm 25:5). He should have waited on this occasion, but he had made up his mind. Given his circumstances, Philistia looked better than the shadow of God's invisible wings.

> So David and the six hundred men with him left and went over to Achish son of Maoch king of Gath. David and his men settled in Gath with Achish. Each man had his family with him, and David had his two wives: Ahinoam of Jezreel and Abigail of Carmel, the widow of Nabal. When Saul was told that David had fled to Gath, he no longer searched for him (1 Samuel 27:2–4).

David hied himself to Philistia and put himself and his army in the service of King Achish. Saul gave up his pursuit, hoping perhaps that David would fall by Philistine hands (1 Samuel 18).

This was the Achish before whom he had embarrassed himself some months before (21:10–15). Now, however,

David was not a solitary refugee but the master of a formidable band of fighting men. David's men were welcome mercenaries. David sold himself into the hands of the Philistines—made himself useful to God's enemies.

Achish no doubt gave David solemn promise of protection, and David and his entourage moved into the royal city.

Ziklag

David was safe in Gath, though increasingly uneasy. His movements were restricted. He had to give up his autonomy and independence. He felt the need to get away from the royal city and so asked Achish for another place to live. It was a modest request:

> Then David said to Achish, "If I have found favor in your eyes, let a place be assigned to me in one of the country towns, that I may live there. Why should your servant live in the royal city with you?"
> So on that day Achish gave him Ziklag, and it has belonged to the kings of Judah ever since. David lived in Philistine territory a year and four months (27:5–7).

Achish had the feudal right to bestow land, and his choice for David was Ziklag. Ziklag lay close to the southern border of the land of Israel—well situated for David's purposes. It had the advantage of being away from Saul's territory and isolated from Gath and other centers of Philistine population.

Ziklag was an Israelite city that had fallen into Philistine hands. It was originally a Canaanite city at first given to the tribe of Judah (Joshua 15:31) and then to Simeon (Joshua 19:5; 1 Chronicles 4:30). The Philistines had seized it, but apparently never inhabited it. It was now abandoned. David and his people moved in bag and baggage.

At last David and his band could settle down. For months their lives had been full of alarm and flight. Now they had a little corner of peace. Their children could play in safety; old men and women could sit in the sun and chat; men could work the fields instead of sustaining themselves by raiding and looting.

David and his people lived in Ziklag unmolested for a time, and everything seemed to be going well outwardly, but this was a barren time in David's walk with God. He wrote no poetry and sang no songs in Ziklag; Israel's sweet singer was mute. David drifted steadily away from the Lord.

But David's drifting did not result in personal failure alone; he also placed his friends in spiritual jeopardy. Philistia lay outside the inheritance of the Lord, the abiding place of the Most High. It was full of idols (2 Samuel 5:21).

Philistine carries with it an entrenched negative image. A *philistine* is someone who is crude, crass, deficient in esthetic sensitivity. But the image is undeserved. The Philistines came from the Aegean Sea and had roots in Greek culture. They were a sophisticated and attractive people.

While in Philistia, David and his followers gained familiarity with Philistine culture and religion. This was a perilous time for those with weaker faith. They were defiled by what they saw.

David's actions tainted Israel for centuries. Israelite men were still attracted to Philistine culture some six hundred years later. They married Philistine women, and their children spoke "the language of Ashdod" (Nehemiah 13:24). They bought into a pagan culture. David was, at least in part, the trendsetter for that declension.

As David drifted away from God he became increasingly restless, a state of mind that always gets us in deep trouble.

Blaise Pascal, a seventeenth-century philosopher, had this to say: "When I have set myself now and then to consider the various distractions of men, the toils and dangers to which they expose themselves in the court or in the camp, whence arise so many quarrels and passions, such daring and often such evil exploits, etc., I have discovered that all these misfortunes of men arise from one thing only, that they are unable to stay quietly in their own chamber . . . . Hence it comes that play, the society of women, war and offices of State are sought after . . . . Hence it comes that men so love noise and movement."

Ah yes. We know.

David's sorties

> Now David and his men went up and raided the Geshurites, the Girzites and the Amalekites. (From ancient times these peoples had lived in the land extending to Shur and Egypt.) Whenever David attacked an area, he did not leave a man or woman alive, but took sheep and cattle, donkeys and camels, and clothes. Then he returned to Achish.
>
> When Achish asked, "Where did you go raiding today?" David would say, "Against the Negev of Judah" or "Against the Negev of Jerahmeel" or "Against the Negev of the Kenites." He did not leave a man or woman alive to be brought to Gath, for he thought, "They might inform on us and say, 'This is what David did.' " And such was his practice as long as he lived in Philistine territory. Achish trusted David and said to himself, "He has become so odious to his people, the Israelites, that he will be my servant for ever" (1 Samuel 27:8–12).

David wasn't content with the quiet life. He was a man of passion and action; he had to mix it up with his enemies.

First Chronicles tells us that men from all the tribes of Israel began to defect from Saul and emigrate to Ziklag and identify with David's cause. "All of them were brave warriors," the chronicler says, "and they were commanders in his army. Day after day men came to help David, until he had a great army, like the army of God" (see 1 Chronicles 12:20–21).

David couldn't waste such resources. From his base in Philistia David began to make sorties into the southern desert against some of Judah's ancient enemies: the Geshurites, Girzites, and the Amalekites. These were aboriginal tribes—Canaanites—who retained control of the land south of Judah, between Judah and Egypt and who were constantly harassing the Israeli settlers in the south. They were allies of the Philistines.

David plundered and looted village after village and distributed the spoils to his kinsmen in Judah: "He sent some of the plunder to the elders of Judah, who were his friends, saying, "Here is a present for you from the plunder of the LORD's enemies" (1 Samuel 30:26).

But there is a jarring note in the narrative: David adopted a policy of extermination—killing men, women, and children, lest they inform on him. The verbs *attacked, leave,* and *took* are what grammarians call "frequentative verbs" describing habitual action. Extermination was his "policy," as the Hebrew text described it, "as long as he lived in Philistine territory." David ran in the fast lane for a year and four months.

A pack of lies

As the king's liege, David was obliged to report on his battles and share some of the booty from his victories. Achish would ask him, "Where did you go raiding today?" David would lie: "I've been raiding Israelites and their allies—the Jerahmeelites and the Kenites."

David embarked on a course that demanded perpetual deceit. He had to keep lying to Achish, a deception utterly unworthy of his character.

Achish accepted David's reports as evidence of his hatred for Israel, thinking David had alienated himself from his countrymen and was now wholly in his service. "He has become odious to his people," he said, "now he will be in my service forever."

Interesting phrase: "He will be in my service forever." David, God's free spirit had sold himself to serve a pagan king. "From wrong to wrong the exasperated spirit proceeds," T. S. Eliot said, "unless restored by that refining fire."

The refining fire

The Philistines gathered their forces at Aphek to go to war against Israel. They were aware of the disintegration of Saul's kingdom and had noted with great satisfaction the growing number of mighty men who were abandoning Saul and identifying themselves with David and, presumably, with themselves.

The Philistines decided to strike a final blow, and so they gathered all their forces—along with David and his mercenaries—with the intent of assaulting Israel across the plain of Esdraelon. David was obliged to follow his king into battle, though he did so with a sinking heart. He knew it meant he must go into battle against his countrymen, against Saul his king and Jonathan his beloved friend.

It may be that at this point David's heart began to turn to God, asking him to extricate him from the mess he had contrived for himself. If so the Lord heard him.

F. B. Meyer has written, "If by your mistakes and sins you have reduced yourself into a false position like this, do not despair; hope still in God. Confess and put away your sin, and humble yourself before Him and he will arise to deliver you. You may have destroyed yourself, but in Him will be your help."

A door of hope was opened. On the eve of the encounter God intervened: the Philistines themselves insisted that David and his men have no part in the battle, and they turned with relief to their homes in Ziklag.

> David and his men reached Ziklag on the third day. Now the Amalekites had raided the Negev and Ziklag. They had attacked Ziklag and burned it, and had taken captive the women and all who were in it, both young and old. They killed none of them, but carried them off as they went on their way.
> When David and his men came to Ziklag, they found it destroyed by fire and their wives and sons and daughters taken captive. So David and his men wept aloud until they had no strength left to weep (30:1–4).

David and his men had been on the road for three days and were exhausted, eagerly anticipating seeing their wives and children.

As they neared Ziklag they saw a plume of smoke on the horizon and ran the last few miles to Ziklag to find the city torched, their women and little ones kidnapped.

Instead of happy reunion there was eerie silence and desolation. There were only a few elderly men and women left to tell the story. David and his men wept until they could weep no more.

David's troops turned and glared at him in angry silence. There was talk of lynching him. David was personally responsible for their loss, and he knew it. He should have left a few men to guard the city. He should have known. He had let his men down. You can imagine his terrible sense of isolation.

And then there was his own personal loss. There was no hope; no human prospect of redeeming the situation. He could never catch the Amalekites. They were mounted on camels and long gone. When you have hope you can endure. When you are robbed of hope, life loses all its meaning.

David sensed the righteous judgment of God. His conscience awoke and began to speak. David had been leading a double life—betraying Achish, raiding Philistine allies. He had massacred whole villages and then had lied. Now his village and family were gone.

This was one of blackest moments in David's life.

David's reaction

David wept in misery and despair. He wept until he could weep no more. A perfectly natural reaction. But the natural is fatal. "By sorrow of the heart the spirit is broken" the proverb says (Proverbs 15:3).

> David was greatly distressed because the men were talking of stoning him; each one was bitter in spirit because of his sons and daughters. But David found strength in the LORD his God (1 Samuel 30:6).

"David was greatly distressed," but he *found strength in the LORD his God.*" The Hebrew text reads, "he strengthened himself in the LORD." That is one of the greatest lines in the Bible.

Once again, David refers to God as *his* God! Doubtless David's men had heard him say repeatedly, "The Lord is *my* shepherd, *my* rock, *my* salvation." Though David had seriously compromised God's name by his failure of faith and by his torturous and treacherous policies, yet the Lord was still *his* God and in the present crisis he could flee to the shelter of his wings.

God never refuses his help, even when we have brought ruin upon ourselves. Regardless of what we have done, we must run to him and take his strong hand. The man who can come to God with the weight of failure on his mind and say to him, "You are my refuge," is the man who understands the gracious heart of God.

Some old saint has said, "Let us make haste—let us not linger to put on any garment, but rush at once in our nakedness, a true child, for shelter from our own mistakes into the salvation of the Father's strong arms."

Then we're told that David "strengthened himself in the LORD." He must have gone back to God's promises of forgiveness and restoration, which so often cheered him at other dark periods of his life. He must have recalled the poems he wrote on other dark days like this that reflected God's faithfulness. He must have remembered that he had been in worse situations than this and that God had greatly helped him in those times. Though his faith had been sorely tested, it had not been disappointed. In this way he encouraged himself.

All around David there was frustration and fear, but God was at hand, "an ever-present help in trouble" (Psalm 46:1). David took strength from God and became a center of peace. Remember Paul's words, "Be a man; be *made* strong" (1 Corinthians 16:13).

David, in the end, recovered everything the Amalekites had stolen, including his family (1 Samuel 30:18), but I must say not all our failures will turn out that way. There are no guarantees in this life that we will get back the family, the business, the reputation we have lost through our foolishness.

We may reach the end of our years a long way from our goals. We may be known more for our failures than for our successes. We may not be powerful or prosperous, but if we accept the disappointment and let it draw us close to God we will find in time that our failure has given us a deeper understanding of his love and grace, and that is by far the better thing.

It requires enormous faith to believe that our failures are for the greater good, but it is true. We learn far more from disappointment than we do from success. We come to know God and his ways. The man who has never failed has never made that discovery.

"Disappointment—His appointment,"
    Change one letter, then I see
That the thwarting of my purpose
    Is God's better choice for me.
His appointment must be blessing,
    Though it may come in disguise,
For the end from the beginning
    Open to His wisdom lies.

"Disappointment—His appointment,"
    Whose? The Lord's, Who loves me best
Understands and knows me fully,
    Who my faith and love would test;
For, like loving earthly parent,
    He rejoices when He knows
That His child accepts, unquestioned,
    All that from His wisdom flows.

"Disappointment—His appointment,"
    "No good thing will He withhold,"
From denials oft we gather
    Treasures of His love untold.
Well He knows each broken purpose
    Leads to fuller, deeper trust,
And the end of all his dealings
    Proves our God is wise and just.

—Annie Johnson Flint

Jonathan

MAKING FRIENDS

A friend is a trusted confidant to whom I am mutually drawn as a companion and ally, whose love for me is not dependent on my performance, and whose influence draws me nearer to the Lord.

—Jerry White

Friendship is one of life's greatest gifts. "Without friends no one would choose to live, though possessed of all other advantages," said Aristotle.

I'll never forget *Brian's Song*, the movie about Gale Sayers' and Brian Piccolo's friendship. Sayers and Piccolo were running backs for the Chicago Bears in 1967–1969. In 1969 Piccolo discovered he had cancer. Despite his efforts to beat the disease and make a comeback, his condition worsened and he died.

The Football Writers Association awarded the George Halas Award that year to Piccolo at their annual banquet in

New York City. Sayers accepted the award for his friend, and when the moment came, he muttered only two sentences: "I accept this award for Brian Piccolo. I *loved* Brian Piccolo."

Such friendships are rare—so rare they're frequently celebrated in story and song. We wonder if *we* will ever find such a friend.

There's an old story that reveals a lot about friendship. It's the account of Jonathan and David's remarkable relationship. In the end David said of Jonathan, "Your love for me was miraculous!"

Affinity

The story of Jonathan and David begins after David's duel with Goliath. As David reported to Jonathan's father, King Saul tells us that "Jonathan became one in spirit with David and he loved him as himself " (1 Samuel 18:1).

Aristotle defined friendship as a "single soul, dwelling in two bodies"—similar to the expression the biblical author uses here, which is literally, "The soul of Jonathan was bonded to the soul of David."

When Jonathan saw David, he felt an immediate affection for him. "He loved him as himself." Jonathan instinctively recognized that he and this long-haired, wild-eyed young man were made of the same stuff: both were outrageous, courageous, go-for-broke men.

We first meet Jonathan in the Bible, when he "smote the Philistine outpost at Geba" (1 Samuel 13:3), an act of rugged heroism that mobilized Israel's paralyzed army.

Next we read about his single-handed assault on a Philistine observation post at Wadi Suweinet (14:1–14). A small enemy unit was located at the top of a cliff overlooking Israel's army and inhibiting their movement. Jonathan "said to the young man bearing his armor, 'Come, let's . . . go over to the outpost of those uncircumcised fellows. Perhaps the LORD will act in our behalf. Nothing can hinder the LORD from saving, whether by many or by few.' 'Do all you have in mind,' his armor-bearer said, 'Go ahead; I am with you heart and soul.' "

The two worked their way up the near-vertical cliff and engaged the Philistines in hand-to-hand combat. As the historian put it, the Philistines "fell before Jonathan, and his armor-bearer . . . ," and the two men drove the soldiers off the top of the cliff.

Jonathan saw David take on the giant, saw his unshakable confidence in God, and recognized a kindred soul. He and David looked at things the same way. This was a man he wanted to be around.

I recall a story about General William Westmoreland who was reviewing a platoon of paratroopers during the Vietnam War. As he went down the line he asked each trooper in turn, "How do you like jumping, son?" "I love it, Sir!" each one bellowed. When he came to the end of the line and asked the final soldier how he liked jumping, the man replied quietly, "I hate jumping, Sir!" "Then why do you jump?" the astonished general asked. "Because I want to be around guys who jump!" he said. That was Jonathan; his man David was a man who "jumped."

A friendship often begins with natural affinity and attraction. We speak of it as "chemistry" as though it's some sort of systemic reaction, but really it's a sharing of common interests and tastes and outlooks on life. You can't force this "knitting" of hearts; it just happens.

Giving

> We can quite well give evidence of friendship,
> and acquire the reputation of kindly feeling,
> without giving anything.

—Blaise Pascal

True relationship, a real friendship is more than friendly words, more than fun, more than affinity. It is giving. "Jonathan made a covenant with David because he loved him as himself. Jonathan took off the robe he was wearing and gave it to David, along with his tunic, and even his sword, his bow and his belt" (18:2–4).

This covenant was a commitment to friendship, initiated by Jonathan. Though a mutual pact, Jonathan was clearly the initiator, binding himself to love David, and sealing the covenant with the gift of his armor.

This is more than Jonathan giving the shirt off his back. Swapping armor was an ancient symbolic token of bonding. The same custom appears in Homer's tales.

The imbalance of an exchange suggests the tilt of the relationship: Jonathan gave away his armor; David had no armor to give. David got Jonathan; Jonathan got nothing in return. Which is exactly the point. As friendship grows, friends give themselves away. Jesus said, "Greater love has no man than that he lays down his life for his friends."

Jonathan was a self-effacing friend. There's no suggestion of self-interest in his friendship. David loved Jonathan and tried to reciprocate the friendship, but his love wasn't subjected to the stresses and strains of Jonathan's love.

Jonathan was forced into a clash of loyalties between father and friend, and he had to face the surrender of his royal station, as well as the fact of David's greater brilliance and popularity. By all the rules, Jonathan should have hated and envied David and bent his efforts to sabotage David's ascent to the throne, but, as the text plainly says, "He loved David as himself." There is no greater love. "It is by loving and not by being loved that one can come nearest to the soul of another," said George McDonald.

Better to love than be beloved
Though lonely all the day.

Better the fountain in the heart,
Than the fountain by the way.

—George MacDonald

Jonathan's befriending was just what David needed at this stage of his life. The tales of the young shepherd boy and the psalms that he later wrote suggest that he was a profoundly disturbed young man—a neglected child, growing up in a cold and hostile environment, often overwhelmed by feelings of inadequacy and depression.

But there's a wonderful healing power in affection. Jonathan loved David, believed in him, and sought God's best for him. It was the environment David needed to grow.

Commitment

You can't stay in your corner of the Forest waiting for others to come to you. You have to go to them sometimes.

—Winnie-the-Pooh

Saul retained David permanently in his service (18:2), and in time Jonathan's love began to pay off. David began shedding his insecurities and showing the stuff of which he was made. "Whatever Saul sent him to do, David did it so successfully that Saul gave him a high rank in the army. This pleased all the people, and Saul's officers as well" (18:5). But it didn't sit well with Saul.

When the men were returning home after David had killed the Philistine, the women came out from all the towns of Israel to meet King Saul with singing and dancing, with joyful songs and with tambourines and lutes. As they danced, they sang:

> "Saul has slain his thousands,
>   and David his tens of thousands."

Saul was very angry; this refrain galled him. "They have credited David with tens of thousands," he thought, "but me with only thousands. What more can he get but the kingdom?" And from that time on Saul kept a jealous eye on David (18:6–9).

Saul's jealousy was what F. B. Meyer called a "hell spark" that should have been trampled under foot, but he let it burn until it turned into white-hot fury that obsessed the king and drove him to try to kill his young rival. Twice, in a fit of rage, he tried to pin David to the wall with his spear, but David evaded him (18:10–11).

The author continues the story with other accounts of palace intrigue and Saul's efforts to do David in by indirect means. Those failing, Saul "told his son Jonathan and all the attendants to kill David" (19:1).

Few of us are ever asked to assassinate a friend, though we may be drawn into efforts to assassinate their character. But Jonathan would not be party to Saul's jealousy:

> Jonathan was very fond of David and warned him, "My father Saul is looking for a chance to kill you. Be on your guard tomorrow morning; go into hiding and stay there. I will go out and stand with my father in the field where you are. [Where he could hear and judge for himself Saul's intentions.] I'll speak to him about you and will tell you what I find out."
>
> Jonathan spoke well of David to Saul his father and said to him, "Let not the king do wrong to his servant David; he has not wronged you, and what he has done has benefited you greatly. He took his life in his hands when he killed the Philistine. The LORD

won a great victory for all Israel, and you saw it and were glad. Why then would you do wrong to an innocent man like David by killing him for no reason?"

Saul listened to Jonathan and took this oath: "As surely as the LORD lives, David will not be put to death."

So Jonathan called David and told him the whole conversation. He brought him to Saul, and David was with Saul as before (19:1–7).

Saul's insanity and instability during this period drove him to extremes of murderous hatred and overwhelming goodwill. This was one of Saul's better days. Jonathan seized the opportunity to bring about a temporary reconciliation.

Jonathan was able to restore David to the court, but shortly after the reconciliation, Saul decided again to rid himself of his rival:

While David was playing the harp, Saul tried to pin him to the wall with his spear, but David eluded him as Saul drove the spear into the wall. That night David made good his escape.

Saul sent men to David's house to watch it and to kill him in the morning. But Michal, David's wife, warned him, "If you don't run for your life tonight, tomorrow you'll be killed." So Michal let David down through a window, and he fled and escaped (19:9–12).

David fled to Samuel, the old prophet, and found sanctuary in his home (19:18). He may have thought that Saul would honor the prophet and leave him alone. But Saul discovered David's hiding place and came after him, and he was once again forced to run.

This time he fled to Jonathan: "What have I done?" he asked. "What is my crime? How have I wronged your father, that he is trying to take my life?" (20:1). Jonathan's naiveté and guilelessness is evident in his answer:

> "You are not going to die! Look, my father doesn't do anything, great or small, without confiding in me. Why would he hide this from me? It's not so!"
>
> But David took an oath and said, "Your father knows very well that I have found favor in your eyes, and he has said to himself, 'Jonathan must not know this or he will be grieved.' Yet as surely as the LORD lives and as you live, there is only a step between me and death" ["one foot in the grave!" we say].
>
> Jonathan said to David, "Whatever you want me to do, I'll do for you" (20:2–4).

As someone has said, "A friend lives to make life less difficult for another."

David reminded Jonathan of their covenant, which he described as a "covenant of the Lord" (20:8), and he appealed to Jonathan to be loyal to that covenant. (The word translated "show kindness" in 20:8 is the same word used for God's loyalty to his covenants with Israel.) In other words, "Stay with me the way God stays with me." He's one who will never leave us or forsake us, and that ought to be the quality of our commitment to one another.

David then devised a plan to determine Saul's inclination:

> "Look, tomorrow is the New Moon festival, and I am supposed to dine with the king; but let me go hide in the field until the evening of the day after tomorrow. If your father misses me at all, tell him, 'David earnestly asked my permission to hurry to Bethlehem, his hometown, because an annual sacrifice is being

made there for his whole clan.' If he says, 'Very well,'
then your servant is safe. But if he loses his temper,
you can be sure that he is determined to harm me. As
for you, show kindness to your servant, for you have
brought him into a covenant with you before the
LORD. If I am guilty, then kill me yourself! Why hand
me over to your father?" (20:5–8).

Jonathan's answer was a vigorous affirmation of David
and promise of loyalty:

"If he is favorably disposed toward you, will I not
send you word and let you know? But if my father is
inclined to harm you, may the LORD deal with me, be
it ever so severely, if I do not let you know and send
you away safely. May the LORD be with you as he has
been with my father. But show me unfailing kindness
like that of the Lord as long as I live, so that I may not
be killed, and do not ever cut off your kindness from
my family—not even when the LORD has cut off
every one of David's enemies from the face of the
earth."
        So Jonathan made a covenant with the house of
David, saying, "May the LORD call David's enemies
to account." And Jonathan had David reaffirm his
oath out of love for him, because he loved him as he
loved himself (20:12–17).

Then Jonathan said,

"The day after tomorrow, toward evening, go to the
place where you hid when this trouble began, and
wait by the stone Ezel. I will shoot three arrows to the
side of it, as though I were shooting at a target. Then I
will send a boy and say, 'Go, find the arrows.' If I say

to him, 'Look, the arrows are on this side of you;
bring them here,' then come, because, as surely as the
LORD lives, you are safe; there is no danger. But if I
say to the boy, 'Look, the arrows are beyond you,'
then you must go, because the LORD has sent you
away. And about the matter you and I discussed—
remember, the LORD is witness between you and me
forever" (20:19–23).

So David hid in the field and when the festival came and
Saul finally realized that Jonathan had sabotaged his efforts to
assassinate David,

> Saul's anger flared up at Jonathan and he said to
> him, "You son of a perverse and rebellious woman!
> Don't I know that you have sided with the son of Jesse
> to your own shame and to the shame of the mother who
> bore you? As long as the son of Jesse lives on this earth,
> neither you nor your kingdom will be established. Now
> send and bring him to me, for he must die!"
> "Why should he be put to death? What has he
> done?" Jonathan asked his father. But Saul hurled his
> spear at him to kill him. Then Jonathan knew that his
> father intended to kill David [a masterpiece of
> understatement]" (20:30–33).

Jonathan stalked out in a rage and in the morning went
out to the field to meet David. Jonathan and the boy acted out
their pre-arranged signal.

> Then Jonathan gave his weapons to the boy and said,
> "Go, carry them back to town."
> After the boy had gone, David got up from the
> south side of the stone and bowed down before
> Jonathan three times, with his face to the ground.

Then they kissed each other and wept together—but
David wept the most.

Jonathan said to David, "Go in peace, for we have
sworn friendship with each other in the name of the
LORD, saying, 'The LORD is witness between you and
me, and between your descendants and my descendants
forever.' " Then David left, and Jonathan went back to
the town (20:40–42).

This is the last of three covenants made between David
and Jonathan. These were the commitments that made their
relationship secure. They supplied the mutual assurance that
neither man would walk out on the other when the going got
tough. They loved each other with the Lord's covenant love:
he will never leave us nor forsake us no matter what we do.

We must love our friends with his love. Shakespeare said,
"Those friends thou hast, and their adoption tried, grapple
them to thy soul with hoops of steel."

The spiritual dimension

Twice in this scene Jonathan refers to their covenant of
friendship as one centered in the Lord (20:23, 42),
introducing the element that makes Christian friendship
unique. Men without God can experience deep friendships
with much caring and giving. They may even lay down their
lives for one another. But the one missing dimension is the
spiritual, and it's that dimension our souls thirst for.

We say that friendship is giving with no strings attached.
The spiritual element of relationship makes that dimension
possible. God's love frees us from inordinate need to *be* loved
in return: "We love because he first loved us," says John
(1 John 4:19). Everyone needs love—it's not good to be
alone—but knowing that we're deeply loved by God frees us
from cursing others with our demands.

The worst friends are those who need us in the worst sort of way. These are the people who break our backs (and our hearts) with their insatiable need to be loved. (A friend once told me that the way to discern demanding love is to see if one's attitude changes when a friend doesn't come through.)

God's love frees us from our compulsive needs to be accepted and loved and befriended, and sets us free to care about others. We may be hurt by coldness and indifference on their part, but we do not have to be controlled by it.

Strengthening one's grip on God

There is one final meeting. David was in exile, hiding in the Desert of Ziph, where "he learned that Saul had come out to take his life." Jonathan went to Horesh and "helped [David] find strength in God. 'Don't be afraid,' he said. 'My father Saul will not lay a hand on you. You will be king over Israel, and I will be second to you. Even my father Saul knows this.' The two of them made a covenant before the LORD. Then Jonathan went home, but David remained at Horesh" (1 Samuel 23:15–18). David never saw Jonathan alive again.

The significance of this scene lies in this: "[Jonathan] helped David find strength in God," or, more literally, "He helped him strengthen his grip on God."

This is the essence of Christian friendship. Beyond common interests, beyond affection, beyond wit and laughter is the ultimate aim of sowing in others the words of eternal life, leaving them with reminders of God's wisdom, refreshing their spirit with words of his love, and strengthening their grip on God.

Untimely death

Saul and Jonathan died together three months later in the battle of Gilboa. "David took up this lament for Saul and his

son Jonathan, and ordered that the men of Judah be taught
this Lament of the Bow (it is written in the Book of Jashar)":

> Your glory, O Israel, lies slain on your heights.
>> How the mighty have fallen!

> Tell it not in Gath, proclaim it not in the streets of
>> Ashkelon,
>> lest the daughters of the Philistines be glad,
>> lest the daughters of the uncircumcised rejoice.

> O mountains of Gilboa, may you have neither dew
>> nor rain,
>> nor fields that yield offerings {of grain}.
> For there the shield of the mighty was defiled,
>> the shield of Saul—no longer rubbed with oil.
> From the blood of the slain, from the flesh of the mighty,
>> the bow of Jonathan did not turn back,
>> the sword of Saul did not return unsatisfied.
> Saul and Jonathan—in life they were loved and gracious,
>> and in death they were not parted.
> They were swifter than eagles, they were stronger
>> than lions.

> O daughters of Israel, weep for Saul, who clothed you
>> in scarlet and finery,
>> who adorned your garments with ornaments of gold.

> How the mighty have fallen in battle! Jonathan lies
>> slain on your heights.
> I grieve for you, Jonathan my brother; you were very
>> dear to me.
> *Your love for me was wonderful, more wonderful than*
>> *that of women.*

How the mighty have fallen! The weapons of war
have perished! (2 Samuel 1:17–27).

"Your love for me was wonderful, more wonderful than
that of women." The Hebrew word here translated "wonderful"
means, "that which awakens awe or astonishment" and is used
mainly of the mighty historic and cosmic acts of God. As
Thoreau said, friendship is "a *divine* league forever struck."

A friendship like that of Jonathan and David is a gift of
God—we must ask God for it and wait. In his time and in his
way he may give us a soul mate.

In the meantime, we can *be* a friend. We can give that gift
to another. As the King James Version put it, "A man that
hath friends must shew himself friendly" (Proverbs 18:24). A
friend is not someone who befriends me, but someone whom
I befriend. The way to make a friend then is to *be* one. With
that perspective in mind, no one needs to be lonely: the world
is full of our friends.

A final word

We long for friends like Jonathan, and it may be that God
will give us that gift. But we must know that even the most
perfect human friendships cannot completely satisfy. "The
human heart has ever craved for a relationship, deeper and
more lasting than any possible among men" says Hugo Black.

The limitations of human affection lead to a larger and
more permanent love. There is a friend who sticks closer than
a brother; we have no greater friend (John 15:13). As Thomas
Aquinas said, we should "love Him and keep Him for thy
Friend, who, when all go away, will not forsake thee, nor
suffer thee to perish at the last."

Abraham

LOSER TAKE ALL

Who overcomes by force hath overcome but half his foe.

—John Milton

Conflict is inevitable. The only people who aren't conflicted are a few isolated lighthouse keepers, Basque sheepherders, Cistercian monks, Salmon River recluses, Sasquatches and other die-hard loners.

If you live in the real world you're going to fall out of phase with someone this week, or, most likely, this day. You can count on it. The question is not how to avoid conflict, but how to manage it.

Moses had a good word on the subject. He tells a story about Abram and his nephew Lot and how Abram resolved their differences. It's another example of how our difficulties can be overcome and turned into good.

The trouble with Abram

The trouble between Abram and Lot began with an agreement to lie. Abraham and Sarah made a promise to one another that they would tell no one they were married whenever his life was on the line (Genesis 20:13).

Sarah was a beautiful woman, and Abram was certain that wherever they went men would covet her and kill him, which was the way things were done back then. If you wanted someone's wife, you made a widow out of her.

So Abraham said to Sarah: "This is the kindness which you will show to me: everywhere we go, say of me, 'He is my brother' " (20:13 NASB).

The lie was a half-truth: Sarah was his half-sister, "the daughter of his mother though not the daughter of his father," as Abraham once lamely explained (20:12). But it was still a lie; Sarah was his wife.

That deceit was Abraham's ace in the hole, his alternative to faith, his fall-back plan in case God didn't come through. But a lie can never grow old; truth inevitably displaces it. Abraham and Sarah were revealed as man and wife, a disclosure that almost cost them their lives.

God, however, whose job it is to undo our stupidity, stepped in and averted the consequences of Abram's lying. As one of Israel's poets put it, he remembered his covenant with Abraham, reproved the king, and would not let him touch his anointed one or do his prophet any harm (Psalm 105:15). It's enough to say that God saved Abram without relying on the patriarch's deceit.

In Egypt Abram gained new perspective. There he learned that though God may ask us to do things that *look* dangerous, he has promised eternal protection, and there is no reason to doubt his word. Our safety never depends on making ourselves safe, but rather on remaining in God's will. That's the safest place in the world.

Back to Bethel

Genesis 13 traces Abram's pilgrimage by stages as he journeyed from Egypt through the Negev back to Bethel:

> So Abram went up from Egypt to the Negev, with his
> wife and everything he had, and Lot went with him. . . .
> And he went on his journey to the place between
> Bethel and Ai where his tent had been earlier and
> where he had first built an altar. There Abram called
> on the name of the LORD (13:1–4).

Abram's pilgrimage was more than a journey through space; it was a walk through time: back to Bethel, all the way back to the origins of his faith.

Bethel was the place where Abram had built his altar "in the beginning," an altar that was conspicuously absent in Egypt. Abram came back to the place of worship where once again he "called on the name of the LORD." It's good that he did. He needed all of God for the trouble that lay ahead.

The problem was too much of a good thing. "Abram had become very wealthy in livestock and in silver and gold" (13:2). Abram was betrayed by his affluence. Sarah's dowry, which the Pharaoh had allowed Abram to keep, set up the subsequent conflict with Lot.

> Lot, who was moving about with Abram, also had
> flocks and herds and tents. But the land could not
> support them while they stayed together, for their
> possessions were so great that they were not able to
> stay together. And quarreling arose between Abram's
> herdsmen and the herdsmen of Lot. The Canaanites
> and Perizzites were also living in the land at that time
> (13:5–7).

Once again the land failed Abram. The first time it failed him through famine. This time there wasn't enough of it to go around. That's what brought Abram and Lot into conflict.

Each time their herdsmen moved their flocks they found themselves in competition with one another and "quarreling arose." That's when the shouting began.

Abram, however, rather than engage in a shouting match with his nephew suggested they sit down and talk about their problem and do something about it:

> Let's not have any quarreling between you and me, or between your herdsmen and mine, for we are brothers (13:8).

"Brothers!" That makes all the difference in the world. Brothers have to get along with one another.

Jesus said, "If you are offering your gift at the altar and there remember that your *brother* has something against you, leave your gift there in front of the altar. First go and be reconciled to your brother; then come and offer your gift. Settle matters quickly with your adversary" (Matthew 5:23–25).

Furthermore, "the Canaanites and Perizzites were *also* living in the land at that time" (13:7). Perhaps, Moses' editorial comment means nothing more than Canaanite competition for grass, but I think he had something else in mind. It was important for Abram to deal with this disunity between brothers because the Canaanites were looking on!

Abram was a missionary. The Lord had said to him,

> Leave your country, your people and your father's household and go to the land I will show you.
> I will make you into a great nation and I will bless you; I will make your name great, and you will be a blessing. I will bless those who bless you, and

whoever curses you I will curse; and *all peoples on earth will be blessed through you* (Genesis 12:1–3).

Abram's task was to bring salvation to the inhabitants of the land. God loved the Canaanites, even though most of them were dirty old men. He wanted these people to see the difference his presence could make in a man. It was important that Abram and Lot settle their differences and manifest God's goodness to the world.

Grace or grass

There is a spate of books and articles these days on conflict management. Many of them contain wisdom, another instance in which "the people of this world are more shrewd in dealing with their own kind than are the people of the light" (Luke 16:8). I find them helpful to read and apply.

To some degree these studies represent an elaboration of Paul's admonition to keep our conversations "full of grace, seasoned with salt" (Colossians 4:6). They help us communicate with grace and sensitivity so that we serve up communication like a savory meal.

But grace adds something more—more than secular studies can ever supply. Once again Jesus' words come to mind: "What are you doing *more* than others?" (Matthew 5:47). Authentic Christianity has that "more than" quality about it. This is the missing element in most secular treatments of this theme.

This is what Abram, God's man, did. He said to Lot,

"Is not the whole land before you? Let's part company. If you go to the left, I'll go to the right; if you go to the right, I'll go to the left."

Lot looked up and saw that the whole plain of the Jordan was well watered, like the garden of the LORD, like the land of Egypt, towards Zoar. (This was before the LORD destroyed Sodom and Gomorrah.) So Lot chose for himself the whole plain of the Jordan and set out toward the east. The two men parted company: Abram lived in the land of Canaan, while Lot lived among the cities of the plain and pitched his tents near Sodom. Now the men of Sodom were wicked and were sinning greatly against the LORD (Genesis 13:9–13).

Abram was the patriarch of the clan and held all the cards. God had given him the title deed to all the land of Canaan (Genesis 12:6). It was his by divine right. Yet he let Lot choose. Abram displayed the humility and generosity of faith.

Lot's choice betrayed his self-interest: He "chose *for himself.*" The Jordan valley looked good on the surface. It was a quiet pastoral scene, but nearby was Sodom, the seductive city that eventually claimed Lot and his family, drew them down and ruined them. There, as Lord Byron pointed out, Lot tasted "the apples on the Dead Sea's shore, All ashes to the taste."

You might conclude at this point that Abram was like one of those men Robert Bly describes as weak, wimpy push-overs. But you'd be wrong. Abram never picked a fight, but he never backed away from one either. When push came to shove, Abram could be fierce.

Shortly after this occasion Lot and his family were captured in a raid on Sodom. Abram armed his household servants and went after them. Never mind that the raiding party was composed of the armies of four of the greatest kings in the Middle East, Abram pursued the invaders through the night, raided their camp, and rescued his nephew Lot (see Genesis 14:1–16).

No, Abram was no soft man. That's not what this story is about. Nor is this a story about grazing rights and grass. It is about grace and God's way to settle our deepest differences.

The fundamental problem

We keep asking ourselves: "How can I find satisfaction?" It's life's fundamental question.

It's not wrong to want satisfaction. God created us with a thousand necessities, and he will see to it that we will get what's coming to us—in this life or the next. He is the source and the satisfaction of our longings.

The problem is not that we want satisfaction; it's that we pursue it as though everything depends on it. If there is any gratification to be gained we must get it.

When we approach problems in this way, our efforts to fulfill ourselves inevitably clash with someone else—a spouse, a child, a colleague—who is trying to fulfill himself or herself, and our drives get frustrated. The person who sabotages us becomes our rival, our obstacle to progress. That person is in our way! We get angry and we refuse to yield.

Disunity comes because we insist on our way and refuse to yield ground. If you look beneath the surface of every divorce, every church split, every dissolution of friendship, you will see this pattern. That's why we can't successfully arbitrate or arrange compromises, except for short periods of time, because our drive for satisfaction sets up a prideful resistance that keeps us at odds with one another. "Only by pride cometh contention," the proverb states, "but with the well advised is wisdom" (Proverbs 13:10 KJV).

Here is wisdom: when conflict cannot be resolved reasonably, when there is no other way to seek reconciliation, we must yield our position even though by so doing we are wronged (see 1 Corinthians 6:1–7). What's called for is what the Bible calls "meekness." Meekness is not weakness or mildness but controlled strength. It is a willingness to give up what we call our rights, our preferences, our privileges in the interests of a better thing. It is a gentle, yielding spirit that meets hard hearts and stubborn wills with quiet forbearance.

When rights are wrong

We have certain inalienable rights. Paul makes that very clear. In his own defense he wrote to the Corinthian church, "Don't we [apostles] have the right to food and drink? Don't we have the right to take a believing wife along with us, as do the other apostles and the Lord's brothers and Cephas? Do not Barnabas and I have a right to refrain from working?" (1 Corinthians 9:4–6).

But, the apostle continues, "We did not use this right. On the contrary, we put up with anything rather than hinder the gospel of Christ" (1 Corinthians 9:12). There are certain times when insisting on rights is dead wrong. In some situations the right thing is to give our rights away and wait for God to satisfy us in some other way.

We're never called upon to sacrifice right principles. "The wisdom that comes from heaven is first *pure*; then peace-loving." We do not seek peace at all costs. Purity always comes first. But when we have reached an impasse in our efforts to reconcile with a brother or sister; when there's nothing more we can do to bring peace, we can yield. The weak have to defend their rights; the strong can yield. This is the grace of giving up.

The God who would be man

Paul has a mind-boggling word on this subject:

Do *nothing* out of selfish ambition or vain conceit, but
in humility consider others better than yourselves.
Each of you should look not only to your own
interests, but also to the interests of others
(Philippians 2:3–4).

Do nothing for yourself? Consider others better than yourself? What a strange doctrine in a world where might makes right and assertiveness makes the man.

This call to humility and self-effacement is so unbelievable, Paul had to corroborate it from the example of Christ. He elaborates from an ancient creed:

> Your attitude should be the same as that of Christ
> Jesus: Who, being in very nature God, did not
> consider equality with God something to be grasped,
> but made himself nothing, taking the very nature of a
> servant, being made in human likeness. And being
> found in appearance as a man, he humbled himself
> and became obedient to death—even death on a cross!
> (Philippians 2:5–8).

This is one of the greatest and most moving descriptions ever given of Jesus, a poetic description of what Christians call the Incarnation—the incredible fact that God himself become a man.

Two ideas appear in the creed, based on the two main verbs: "[Jesus] made himself nothing" ("he *emptied* himself") and "he humbled himself" (2:8).

Jesus was always God. He never ceased to be God at any time. But, as Paul explains, he "did not consider equality with God something to be grasped," but "emptied himself." The word means just that; it was used in ancient times of emptying containers, pouring out their contents until nothing was left.

The next verb describes and explains that emptying. Jesus "emptied himself [by] taking the very nature of a servant." The word for "nature" here is the same word used in verse 6: "Who, being in very *nature* God, did not consider equality with God something to be grasped. . . ." The two nouns link two ideas together: he who was essentially God took on the essential nature of a slave.

And then, having become a servant to all, our Lord "humbled himself and became obedient to death—even death on a cross!" Jesus' willingness to serve us sent him all the way. This "mind" as Paul calls it, must be our mind-set as well.

It is in giving that we receive; it is in dying that we live.

—St. Francis of Assisi

Here's the rub: when we face some hard-headed antagonist who will not back down, will we follow our natural instincts and fight back, or will we adopt Jesus' attitude and yield? If we are God's men, we will waive our rights and yield. But not to worry. God will pay us back by the oldest and oddest paradox in the world: we gain ground by giving up.

Jesus said, "Whoever finds his life will lose it, and whoever loses his life for my sake will find it" (Matthew 10:39). If we set out to find ourselves—if we seek our own satisfaction—we will always be left with an empty and unfulfilled heart. Only when we forget ourselves and devote ourselves to another's fulfillment will we find our own souls running over with satisfaction. This is one of the fundamental mysteries of life, but it is confirmed every day.

When Jesus gave in

God *exalted him to the highest place* and gave him the name that is above every name, that at the name of Jesus every knee should bow, in heaven and on earth and under the earth, and every tongue confess that Jesus Christ is Lord, to the glory of God the Father (Philippians 2:9–11).

God exalts the humble, Peter insists (1 Peter 5:5). It was true for Jesus; it was true for Abram.

The LORD said to Abram after Lot had parted from him, "Lift up your eyes from where you are and look

north and south, east and west. All the land that you
see I will give to you and your offspring forever. I
will make your offspring like the dust of the earth, so
that if anyone could count the dust, then your
offspring could be counted. Go, walk through the
length and breadth of the land, for I am giving it to
you" (Genesis 13:14–17).

After Lot's claim came God's grant. The Lord showed
Abram the Promised Land in panorama, then told him to
possess it: "Go, walk through the length and breadth of the
land," an ancient symbolic rite by which Abram staked a
personal claim to his estate. A walk of faith indeed! Abram
grasped for himself "how wide and long and high and deep is
the love of Christ" (Ephesians 3:18).

Lot chose for himself and lost everything in the world;
Abram let God choose and he got the earth with heaven
thrown in. As martyred missionary Jim Elliot wrote, "He is
no fool who gives what he cannot keep to gain what he
cannot lose."

Do we dare?

But you say, "If I do not stand up for my rights, I'll lose
out." So what? You may lose a few of your possessions,
perhaps a little prestige and position, but you'll not be a loser.
The Lord is standing by; he will never permit you to suffer
eternal loss. He will compensate you for all you have lost
through courtesy and kindness. And he is here now to give
you peace and satisfaction for the present.

"I tell you the truth," Jesus said, "no one who has [given
up anything for my sake] will fail to receive many times as
much in this age and, in the age to come, eternal life" (Luke
18:30). That comes from the One who cannot lie.

T. S. Eliot wrote these provocative and challenging lines:

Do we dare? do we dare?
Is it time to climb the stair?

Do we dare to try this radical high road to conflict resolution? Are we willing to give up to gain a greater thing? Do we dare? Do we dare?

Caleb

FINISHING STRONG

He died climbing.

—Epitaph on a Swiss guide's tombstone

There is a naiveté among young people that leads them to think that old people have always been old. Further-more, they think that they themselves will never get old.

I understand the delusion. When I was young I sincerely believed that because I jogged, lifted weights, and ate right my body would go on forever. But I can tell you it isn't so. Every body descends into decay.

The old philosopher had it exactly right:

When the keepers of the house [the hands] tremble,
and the strong men [legs] stoop,
when the grinders [teeth] cease because they are few,

and those looking through the windows [eyes]
　　grow dim;
when the doors to the street [ears] are closed
　　and the sound of grinding fades;
when men rise up at the sound of birds,
　　but all their songs grow faint;
when men are afraid of heights
　　and of dangers in the streets;
when the almond tree blossoms [hair]
　　and the grasshopper drags himself along
　　and desire no longer is stirred . . . (Ecclesiastes
12:3–5).

In my opinion, the first half of life is a piece of cake. The last half is hard. Old age is not for sissies. It takes a strong man to stick the landing.

I must also say, however, that there is good in aging. In the first place, you don't have to prove anything anymore. You can sit on the sidelines and watch other men jockey for position. Like Shakespeare's octagenarian, King Lear, you can kick back as you "pray and sing and tell old tales."

Another advantage of aging is that it breaks down your energy and strength, and prevents you from too much activity. It's God's way of telling you to slow down and take more time for him. "Time hath a taming hand," John Henry, Cardinal Newman once wrote.

Paul said of himself, "Therefore we do not lose heart. Though outwardly we are wasting away, yet inwardly we are being renewed day by day" (2 Corinthians 4:16). If we, like the apostle, take advantage of the aging process, we can stay spiritually strong and vital to the end, "green and full of sap," as the psalmist said.

Occasionally you come across some old-timer who understands these things, who seems to be in touch with something the rest of the pack have lost track of. Caleb, the son of Jephunah, was just such a man.

At 85 years of age, when most of his peers had retired to their condos by the Red Sea, old Caleb kept on truckin'. He went for the highest and the best—Mount Hebron, where the Anakim dwelled.

The beginning of the story

We first meet Caleb at Kadesh, Israel's staging point for their long-awaited campaign against the Canaanites. There the Israelites made their first mistake: they sent spies into the land to gather intelligence.

It's true the impulse seemed to come from God, but that was his concession to their unbelief. Forty years later Moses would say, "All of you came to me and said, 'Let us send men ahead to spy out the land for us and bring back a report about the route we are to take and the towns we will come to' " (Deuteronomy 1:22).

It was a profound mistake. God had promised to give them the land. He knew Canaan like the back of his hand. Why did his people need to gather intelligence? Why were they so anxious to make their own assessment? Couldn't they trust his judgment? It was bad decision based on that old assumption that in general men know better then God.

And so, because God gives all men the right to be wrong, he let Israel have what they wanted. He said to Moses, "Send some men to explore the land of Canaan, which I am giving to the Israelites. From each ancestral tribe send one of its leaders" (Numbers 13:2).

Moses selected twelve choice young men. Their names are supplied in the verses that follow (13:4–16). Of the twelve, only two are memorable: Hoshea (whom Moses renamed Joshua) and Caleb. All the rest were unremarkable, easily forgotten, well known for being unknown.

Joshua we know well. Caleb is less familiar. He was an unusual fellow. First, his name means "dog"—a nickname, most likely. Dogs back then were not pets, but wild, feral creatures noted more for their ferocity than for being man's best friend. Caleb's name suggests that, at least at one point of his life, he was as mean as a junkyard dog.

The other thing about Caleb is that he was a Kenizzite, not an Israelite. The Kenizzites were a wild tribe of nomads that ranged throughout the Sinai and southern Palestine.

Caleb was a pariah, an outsider who, by God's grace, had come in from the cold.

The expedition

Moses sent out twelve spies with these instructions:

"Go up through the Negev and on into the hill country. See what the land is like and whether the people who live there are strong or weak, few or many. What kind of land do they live in? Is it good or bad? What kind of towns do they live in? Are they unwalled or fortified? How is the soil? Is it fertile or poor? Are there trees on it or not? Do your best to bring back some of the fruit of the land" (Numbers 13:17–20).

The spies explored the land from the Wilderness of Zin in the south to Rehob at Lebo-hamath, two hundred fifty miles to the north. They discovered that Canaan was, as God had said, a land flowing with milk and honey. But the Canaanites were there, and their cities were strongly fortified.

Also, the Anakim were there, the Titans of Mount Hebron, whose stature and strength were legendary. These were the gigantic men of whom the proverb was written, "Who can stand up against the Anakites?" (Deuteronomy 9:2).

The spies spent forty days reconnoitering Canaan, at the end of which time they returned to Israel's encampment and made their report:

"We went into the land to which you sent us, and it does flow with milk and honey! Here is its fruit. But the people who live there are powerful, and the cities are fortified and very large. We even saw descendants of Anak there. The Amalekites live in the Negev; the Hittites, Jebusites and Amorites live in the hill country; and the Canaanites live near the sea and along the Jordan" (Numbers 13:27–29).

Up to this point all twelve spies were in perfect agreement. This was an accurate portrayal of the situation. Then the ten said,

"We can't attack those people; they are stronger than we are . . . . The land we explored devours those living in it. All the people we saw there are of great size. We saw the Nephilim there (the descendants of Anak come from the Nephilim). We seemed like grasshoppers in our own eyes, and we looked the same to them" (Numbers 13:30–33).

The people sided with the ten, and Moses had a mutiny on his hands.

That night all the people of the community raised their voices and wept aloud. All the Israelites grumbled against Moses and Aaron, and the whole assembly said to them, "If only we had died in Egypt! Or in this desert! Why is the LORD bringing us to this land only to let us fall by the sword? Our wives and children will be taken as plunder. Wouldn't it be better for us to go back to Egypt?" (Numbers 14:1–3).

Moses and Aaron fell on their faces, but Joshua and Caleb rose to the occasion:

"The land we passed through and explored is exceedingly good. If the LORD is pleased with us, he will lead us into that land, a land flowing with milk and honey, and will give it to us. Only do not rebel against the LORD. And do not be afraid of the people of the land, because we will swallow them up. Their protection is gone, but the LORD is with us. Do not be afraid of them (Numbers 14:7–9).

There's a lot of talk in this chapter about giant people and impossible places. All twelve of the spies had seen the strength of the Canaanites and the size of their walled cities, but Caleb and Joshua had a different way of looking at things.

The ten said, "We can't attack these people!" The two said, "We can!" We can't! We can! All the difference in the world.

What made the difference? The ten compared the giants with themselves and the giants loomed large; the two compared the giants with God and the giants were cut down to size. "The LORD is with us," they said. "We have no reason to be afraid!"

Unbelief never gets beyond the difficulties—the impregnable cities and the impossible giants. It preoccupies itself with them, brooding over them, pitting them against mere human resources.

Faith, on the other hand, though it never minimizes the dangers and difficulties of any circumstance, looks away from them to God and counts on his invisible presence. "The LORD is with us," Caleb insisted, "do not be afraid of the giants."

The book of Hebrews echoes the same sentiment: "God has said, 'I will never leave you; I will never forsake you.' So we say with confidence, 'The Lord is my helper; I will not be afraid. What can man do to me?' " (Hebrews 13:5–6).

What are your "giants"? A habit you cannot break? A temptation you cannot resist? A difficult marriage from which there is no escape? An overbearing boss? A rebellious son or daughter for whom there are no answers?

If we compare ourselves with our difficulties we will always be overwhelmed. But if we compare them with God there is nothing we cannot do. Faith looks away from the greatness of the undertaking to the greatness of an ever-present, all-powerful God.

The Panama Canal builders originated the so-called impossibilities song. Somehow it found its way into some of our chorus books, altered to express a faith that sees every difficulty as an opportunity for God to show himself strong.

> *Got any rivers you think are uncrossable?*
> *Got any mountains you can't tunnel through?*
> *God specializes in things thought impossible;*
> *And He can do what no other power can do.*

We can't; he can. Therefore, we can. "I can do everything through him who gives me strength" (Philippians 4:13)

The promise

Despite Caleb's counsel of faith, the people picked up rocks to stone him, but God intervened and in wrath God swore to himself that not one of that generation would enter the land. The writer of Hebrews concludes, "We see that they could not enter in because of unbelief" (Hebrews 3:19).

But there were two notable exceptions: Joshua, the son of Nun, and Caleb, the son of Jephunneh.

"Because my servant Caleb has a different spirit and follows me wholeheartedly, I will bring him into the land he went to, and his descendants will inherit it" (Numbers 14:24).

The vow and its exception is repeated later:"Because they [the Israelites] have not followed me wholeheartedly, not one of the men twenty years old or more who came up out of Egypt will see the land I promised on oath to Abraham, Isaac and Jacob—not one except Caleb son of Jephunneh the Kenizzite and Joshua son of Nun, for they followed the LORD wholeheartedly" (32:10–12).

The spies who brought the discouraging word died in the wilderness, but "Joshua son of Nun and Caleb son of Jephunneh survived" (14:38).

For forty years Caleb waited while that generation died off. For forty years he counted the days, counting on the promise, waiting for his chance. Like Milton's Abdiel, Caleb was "faithful among the faithless, only faithful he."

Caleb's inheritance

Forty-five years later, Caleb got his chance. The story is told in the book of Joshua.

Under Joshua's leadership Israel invaded Canaan, and in a series of lightning strikes they conquered the major strongholds in the land. The back of Canaanite resistance was broken, but there were still large areas of the land to be claimed.

All Israel gathered at Gilgal to determine which tribes would secure those unconquered regions, but before the first lot was drawn, Caleb stepped forward to claim his piece of ground:

> "You know what the LORD said to Moses the man of God at Kadesh Barnea about you and me. I was forty years old when Moses the servant of the LORD sent me from Kadesh Barnea to explore the land. And I brought him back a report according to my convictions, but my brothers who went up with me made the hearts of the people sink. I, however, followed the LORD my God wholeheartedly. So on

day Moses swore to me, 'The land on which your feet have walked will be your inheritance and that of your children for ever, because you have followed the Lord my God wholeheartedly.'

"Now then, just as the Lord promised, he has kept me alive for forty-five years since the time he said this to Moses, while Israel moved about in the desert. So here I am today, eighty-five years old! I am still as strong today as the day Moses sent me out; I'm just as vigorous to go out to battle now as I was then. Now give me this hill country that the Lord promised me that day. You yourself heard then that the Anakites were there and their cities were large and fortified, but, the Lord helping me, I will drive them out just as he said."

Then Joshua blessed Caleb son of Jephunneh and gave him Hebron as his inheritance. So Hebron has belonged to Caleb son of Jephunneh the Kenizzite ever since, because he followed the Lord, the God of Israel, wholeheartedly. (Hebron used to be called Kiriath Arba after Arba, who was the greatest man among the Anakites.)

Then the land had rest from war (Joshua 14:6–15).

We can infer from Caleb's speech that the spies did not travel together, but were distributed individually throughout Canaan, each one searching a particular portion of the land. Caleb's portion was Hebron, the haunt of the dreadful Anakim.

If this is true it gives a special flair and audacity to Caleb's faith. He had personally reconnoitered Hebron, the habitat of the giants, and had seen them in their natural setting and strength. And yet he longed for that land.

It also gives special meaning to the land-grant made to him then and there: "On that day," he said, "Moses swore to me, 'The land on which your feet have walked will be your inheritance and that of your children for ever' " (Joshua 14:9). This was a promise that by God's grace he would take the high ground.

Caleb asked for no soft spot on which to retire, but the rugged places where the fierce and terrible Anakim dwelled. When most men would have sought retirement, old Caleb kept on truckin'.

We ask, "What made this ancient veteran so aggressive and young at heart? What kept him on the cutting edge?" Six times we're told, "He followed the LORD, the God of Israel, wholeheartedly."

He wholly followed the Lord

The expression "follow the LORD wholeheartedly" means simply that: Caleb followed the Lord *wholeheartedly*. He kept on walking with him, talking with him, worshiping him, loving him, listening to him, "trying to learn what is pleasing to the LORD."

He kept wanting what God wanted, willing what God willed, and so continued into old age to be the embodiment of God's every thought, the expression of his every desire. Caleb never gave up in his pursuit of God, and that's what kept him young at heart.

How striking are the last lines that David Livingstone penned on the night that his sons found him dead on his knees beside his bed in an attitude of prayer, a candle burning beside him: "My Jesus, my king, my life, my all; to Thee again I dedicate myself." He never gave up; every day was another day to grow.

David said, "This God is our God for ever and ever; he will be our guide *even to the end*" (Psalm 48:14). It's especially important to remember this truth as we grow older. We tend to lose heart as we age. Very few motives are capable of operating then. Our physical strength abates; our health deteriorates; our memory gets cloudy. As a friend of mine used to say, "Just about the time your face clears up, your mind starts to go."

But Paul assures us, we need not lose heart. "Though outwardly we are wasting away, yet inwardly we are being renewed day by day" (2 Corinthians 4:16). Every day can be a new beginning toward "good old age." It can mean maturing, growing in grace, and becoming more like Jesus, getting sweeter as the days go by—more mellow, less critical of others, less impatient with the young and with their peculiarities. We don't judge them just because they're different.

There's something exquisitely manly about an older man, "stayed upon Jehovah," filled with his presence and redolent with his fragrance.

> The righteous will flourish like a palm tree,
>   they will grow like a cedar of Lebanon;
> planted in the house of the LORD,
>   they will flourish in the courts of our God.
> They will still bear fruit in old age,
>   they will be full of sap and very green (Psalm 92:12–14).

The drain of the years is amply met by the spring of God's grace that flows within. There is no reason to decline as we age. "The last sheaves that fall beneath thy sickle can be the heaviest; the width of thy swath can be the greatest as you turn toward home," said F. B. Meyer.

Getting older can mean growing, maturing, serving, ministering, venturing, enjoying ourselves to the end of our days. There is still service to be rendered, mountains to be climbed, Anakim to be routed. "Old men ought to be explorers," insists T. S. Eliot. "Have a blast while you last," a friend of mine contends.

Many men approach their senior years and stagnate. They don't just get old; they get obsolete. "I've paid my dues," they say; "I've done my share. Let younger men lead." But none of us will ever have done our share. We can never repay the debt of love we owe to our Lord for what he has done for us.

True, as we age we may not have enough strength and endurance for frontline leadership. Even God made provision for priests in Israel to retire at age 50 from the more physically demanding work connected with the daily sacrifices. But they did not retire from ministry. They continued to walk with God and pass on their wisdom to others.

Those who make retirement the chief end of man wither and die before their time. You see them around town sitting on park benches—dull, dreary old men with nothing to do. They have that dead look in their eyes. Grown old in a weary world, "no wonder waits them," said Byron.

A friend of mine, Ron Ritchie, claims that more people die in Winnebagos than any other vehicle. I think he has something there. Most people die as soon as they retire—if not in their bodies at least in their souls. Yogi Berra observed that "a lot of people my age are dead at the present time."

Not so Caleb. There was no stagnation in him. "What he greatly thought he nobly dared." Caleb thrashed the giants—Sheshai, Ahiman, and Talmai—and drove them from the summit. He did what the rest of Israel could not and would not do, and he did it at age eighty-five because "he wholly followed the Lord."

I think of some lines from Alfred, Lord Tennyson . . .

We are not now that strength which in old days
Moved heaven and earth; but that which we are,
*   we are:*
One equal temper of heroic hearts,

Made weak by time and fate, but strong in will
To strive, to seek, to find, and not to yield.

"To strive, to seek, to find, and not to yield"—a fitting epitaph for Caleb, and for us. Everything in us may beg us to back off, go slow, take it easy, lay back, and leave well enough alone, but that's old folk's talk. Those who walk with God never give up. They die climbing!

Moving on

Hebron is not the end of the story. From there Caleb soldiered on.

> [Caleb] marched against the people living in Debir (formerly called Kiriath Sepher). And Caleb said, "I will give my daughter Acsah in marriage to the man who attacks and captures Kiriath Sepher." Othniel son of Kenaz, Caleb's brother, took it; so Caleb gave his daughter Acsah to him in marriage.
> One day when she came to Othniel, she urged him to ask her father for a field. When she got off her donkey, Caleb asked her, "What can I do for you?"
> She replied, "Do me a special favor. Since you have given me land in the Negev, give me also springs of water." So Caleb gave her the upper and lower springs (Joshua 15:15–19).

Debir was originally called Kiriath Sepher, the "City of Books," so called because it was a depository of the books and learning of the Anakim, the fountainhead of that degraded, dangerous culture.

Debir had been conquered once before but had fallen again into Canaanite hands (see Joshua 10:39). Caleb was determined to wrest it once and for all from their control.

He did not himself engage in the struggle; rather he stirred up his nephew. It was "Othniel son of Kenaz, Caleb's brother, [who] took it" (Joshua 15:17)—the same Othniel who later became the first judge of Israel—the brave champion who saved Israel from Cushan-Rishathaim, the king of Aram (Judges 3:9–10).

Older folks may not have the energy or inclination for leadership, but they are an invaluable asset to the next generation. Their greatest usefulness lies in passing on their faith and their wisdom to others.

Not all old-timers are wise, of course. There are wise old men and there are wicked old men. But since knowledge, wisdom, and character is cumulative, those who have loved God and walked with him through time reach maturity rich in their understanding of God and wise in his ways.

It is then that they can have a powerful influence on other men, especially younger men. They become the saints and sages of whom Robert Bly speaks, the wise old men who can pass on the sacred truths and the solemn secrets.

To idle away our last years in self-indulgence and indolence is to rob ourselves and others of the best years of our lives. Even when "old and gray," we can declare "[God's] power to the next generation, [his] might to all who are to come" (Psalm 71:18). No one yet has ever outlived his usefulness.

Make us Thy mountaineers:
We would not linger on the lower slope,
Fill us afresh with hope, O God of Hope,
That undefeated we may climb the hill
As seeing Him who is invisible.

Let us die climbing. When this little while
Lies far behind us, and the last defile
Is all alight, and in that light we see
Our Leader and our Lord, what will it be?

—Amy Carmichael

Note to the Reader

The publisher invites you to share your response to the message of this book by writing Discovery House Publishers, Box 3566, Grand Rapids, MI 49501, USA. For information about other Discovery House books, music, or videos, contact us at the same address or call 1-800-653-8333. Find us on the Internet at http://www.dhp.org/ or send e-mail to books@dhp.org.